READ-ALOUD PLAYS ABOUT

THE CIVIL WAR

by Timothy Nolan

SCHOLASTIC
PROFESSIONAL BOOKS

NEW YORK • TORONTO • LONDON • AUCKLAN
MEXICO CITY • NEW DELHI • HONG K

Like all my work, this book is dedicated to my wonderful wife Susannah, and to my beautiful daughter Olivia Rose, that she may know and love the history of her country.

Cover design by Jaime Lucero
Cover photography reproduced from the collection of the Library of Congress (2 center photos), and the Massachusetts Historical Society (right).
Interior Design by Mindy Belter
Interior Illustration by Mona Mark

ISBN 0-590-02897-9

Printed in the U.S.A.

Table of Contents

INTRODUCTION

The People Are the History

The Civil War, the War Between the States, the War for Southern Independence. The great and horrible conflict that took place between 1861 and 1865—the last major war fought on American soil—is known by many names. The Civil War is considered by some historians to be the turning point in our nation's history because it marks the point when the United States of America was no longer a "noble experiment" or a collection of individual states with individual agendas but truly had become a nation.

And yet, like all events in history, the story of the Civil War is a really a series of smaller stories and events. It is stories of people caught up in events of the moment, events usually not of their own making, events that forced them to take some sort of action, for example:

- *The greatest general on either side of the Civil War (and some say the greatest general this nation has ever produced) was Robert E. Lee, who fought with valor, courage, and extraordinary intelligence in the Mexican War. Many historians believe that if Lee had led the Union armies, the war could have been over in less than a year. Lee, however, felt compelled by his own moral code and upbringing to stand by his native state of Virginia. That single, very personal decision may have cost the country four years of war.*

- *The Battle of Gettysburg is often cited as the turning point of the war. As the bloody battle was in its third day, and its final charge up Cemetery Ridge failed, the Confederate army was decimated by casualties, fueled by chaos and confusion, and on the run. Yet the Union general, George G. Meade, having repulsed the attacking Confederates, could not bring himself to follow Lee's army back into Virginia and after the three brutal days of fighting, Meade's action, or inaction, created a pause in the fight and gave General Lee what he needed most—time, time to reorganize his army and continue the fight.*

- *An actor, and Southerner, couldn't bring himself to join the Confederate army and fight. Yet John Wilkes Booth's never—ending thirst for glory might have cost his beloved South the best friend it had in Washington. After Booth's assassination of Lincoln, the tide of Reconstruction turned in favor of those who wanted to impose a hard peace on the South, the effects of which are still being felt today.*

In many ways, the dramatic form is the perfect medium for showing the "story in history." While we cannot reproduce exact dialogue or fully recreate historical events, drama does allow you, your students, and other participants to see and feel

 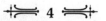

the actions and emotions of the men and women involved in what were seminal moments in American history—and how those actions and emotions created the events we study today.

With this book of plays, we hope to increase classroom opportunities by presenting some events of the Civil War in a cross-curricular context. By dramatizing the personal stories of men and women involved in the Civil War—episodes of their lives, how they saw or participated in these events—it is the author's hope that these men and women, who in large and small ways left their mark on our history, will be seen as people, and students will not only identify them as Americans but identify with them as Americans.

The Purpose of the Plays and Activities

These readers' theater plays are intended to enhance classroom learning in many ways. By taking a cross-curricular approach, we hope to increase opportunities for you to integrate these plays into your curriculum. These plays can enhance classroom learning as a:

• method of increasing appreciation and knowledge of our American heritage

• reading activity

• way to build oral literacy

• chance for increasing class involvement

• way of encouraging appreciation for theater and acting

• writing prompt

• way of involving at-risk or withdrawn students

• whole-class interactive learning activity

How To Use This Book

Reading aloud plays is one of the most effective ways to promote literacy and history in your classroom. We encourage you to invite students to perform these plays as part of your reading, language arts, or social studies curriculum. Before you begin, encourage readers to spend a few moments reading over their lines and getting acquainted with the characters they are playing.

Casting Every effort has been made to have many characters as possible in each play, including important characters for both boys and girls. However, don't feel limited by traditional roles. Non-traditional casting can help forge the connection between students and their American heritage.

Preparation and predicting It will enhance students' educational experience, not to mention their understanding and enjoyment, if you use a prediction exercise before the reading. Ask students if they have ever heard of the event or central figure in the play (most have heard of Robert E. Lee, but few may have heard of Mary Chestnut) and what they know about him or her.

A GREAT PREDICTING ACTIVITY

The night before reading the play in class, direct each student to
find one fact about the event or person featured in the play.
Then have them bring their facts into class for discussion.
Discuss their facts. This will give students something to listen
for (prediction and confirmation).

Historical background and bibliography Each play is followed by historical background which provides a context for the events and which can used as jumping-off point for discussion questions and activities. The bibliography contains a variety of books, nonfiction and fiction, that pertain directly to the event or the themes of each play.

Discussion questions The discussion questions are designed to be used immediately after the play has been read. The questions allow the students to process and reflect on what they have just read and also reinforce the themes and historical facts that have been presented. They also help set the stage for the activities.

Activities At the end of each play are four classroom activities. The activities are meant to be used in conjunction with the plays, but by no means should you limit your discussion or lesson to what is presented. Feel free to tailor and extend the activities to appeal to the interests of your students.

Many of the activities ask for students to present research to the class. As one of our stated purposes is to promote literacy, especially oral literacy, encourage students to present their reports to the class whenever possible and the rest of the class to ask questions. You may find that expecting all your students to participate as speakers and listeners will foster an atmosphere of mutual respect. The more you do this, the more comfortable your students will become in presenting their work to the group, and the greater pride they will take in their work.

You can take the activities one step further by having the students write their own dramas. Try having them write the same episodes from different points of view or create "next day" plays—plays that continue the story.

Encourage re-enactments or role-playing games. Try assigning different historical roles to students and having them research their roles so they really begin to understand who they are playing. Hold the historical re-enactments in class. Do not limit students to lines and scripts, rather have them rely on their research and recall to enact their roles. Students will not only learn research and recall skills, but will develop confidence in themselves and their ability to learn, and to see the value of history.

Performances You may be surprised by how enthusiastic your students are about reading the plays. As a way of encouraging and nurturing their enthusiasm, think about other ways of performing the plays. For instance, if you find your class is hungry for more performances, take the plays before the whole school—organized around a holiday, historical theme, or personal connections. Inspire parents to get involved by donating or making costumes, building sets, making posters, and promoting publicity. You will find that presenting the plays can be done cheaply and without much trouble—students can paint sets on large poster paper which can then be hung at the back of the stage; cast-off clothing can become a period costume. This can be a great way to celebrate Women's History Month, Black History Month, President's Week, or historical anniversaries such as the firing on Fort Sumter or the surrender at Appomattox.

I hope you enjoy these scenes from our nation's heritage.

—TN

THE SOUTH BREAKS AWAY

Mary Chestnut and Her Diary

CAST
(in order of appearance)

First Narrator

Second Narrator

Anne Scott: Friend of the Chestnuts

Mary Chestnut: Southern woman; writer

Charles Lewis Scott: Anne's husband, former member of U.S. Congress

Clara Jansen: Northern woman

Varina Davis: First Lady of the Confederacy

James C. Chestnut: Mary's husband; former U.S. Senator

Maria Whitaker: Mary's slave

Laurence: Chestnuts' slave

Julia Toombs: Mary's friend

Louisa Hamilton: Neighbor of the Chestnuts in Charleston

Louis T. Wigfall: Former U.S. Senator; secessionist

SCENE ONE

This scene takes place in March 1861 in the parlor of a hotel in
Montgomery, Alabama.

FIRST NARRATOR: It is 1861. Abraham Lincoln has been elected president of the United States. One of the goals of his party, the Republican Party, is to end slavery. As a result of Lincoln's election, Southern states have begun seceding from the Union to form their own nation. Many Southerners in the U.S. Congress, like James C. Chestnut, resigned from their offices. They left Washington, D.C., to return home.

SECOND NARRATOR: When a state secedes, it decides that it would be better off running its own affairs rather than being part of the United States. In the case of the Southern states, they felt that the North, which was industrial, didn't understand the agricultural way of in the South. The South felt the North was imposing rules that would hurt their economy and culture. Much of the talk, in both the North and the South, was about what would happen between the two sides.

ANNE SCOTT: Lincoln, you know, despite his appearance, is the cleverest Yankee type there is. Ugly as sin, you know, always sitting on boxes at the country store, telling the most awful—the funniest—stories and whittling away with a knife.

MARY CHESTNUT: Mr. Douglas of Illinois confided to my husband that Lincoln was the hardest fellow to handle that he'd ever met. And Lincoln surely did hammer Mr. Douglas into the ground in the debates.

CHARLES LEWIS SCOTT: Mark my words, if this country can be joked and laughed out of its right, then Lincoln's the man to do it. Let's just see what happens if there's a war, and Yankee pockets get pinched instead of filled—

CLARA JANSEN *(overhearing and interrupting):* Northerners are no more mean and stingy than Southerners, sir!

CHARLES LEWIS SCOTT: My apologies, of course, ma'am. You're quite correct. Northerners and Southerners share the same vices and virtues.

CLARA JANSEN: You will *try* to make war based on Mr. Lincoln's appearance, but that will not do! We know what this is all about! Slavery, pure and simple!

MARY CHESTNUT: On the contrary, there's nothing simple about it. Think of the North and the South as having different temperaments. We are incompatible in so many ways—climate, economy, geography, society—we must divorce each other. But let's not fight about it. Let each of us go our separate ways and say no more about it.

CLARA JANSEN: *I* hold my tongue, Mrs. Chestnut, you know that I do, but what am I to do when I, a Northern woman, am attacked? Why, just this morning, I was playing "Yankee Doodle" on the piano and the judge came in and asked me to leave out the Yankee while I played the Doodle!

(The others can't hide their laughter, and she stalks out.)

MARY CHESTNUT: We *are* terrible. Poor woman, if I were up North, I would expect them to argue against the South—and I would hold my tongue.

VARINA DAVIS: You were until quite recently in the North, Mrs. Chestnut, as was I, until our husbands resigned from Congress. As I recall, you did not always hold your tongue.

MARY CHESTNUT: No, but I knew that I should, and I felt quite sorry about it.

VARINA DAVIS *(sighing):* You are quite right about Southern and Northern temperaments. Heading the Confederate armies as general would have suited my husband so much better than being president of the Confederacy. People are so hard to please. You should have seen his face when he received the telegram telling him that he'd been elected. You would have thought his best friend had died.

ANNE SCOTT: Still, it may not come to war, you know.

CHARLES LEWIS SCOTT: It may not, but if it should—the South is ready.

MARY CHESTNUT: Are we?

SECOND NARRATOR: That night Mary wrote in her diary.

MARY *(as she writes):* Tonight . . . we talked of ourselves and the North. We only want to separate from them, and yet they put such an inordinate value on us, they are willing to risk all. We are like an unwilling bride. I think incompatibility of temper began when it was made plain to us that we get all the problems of slavery and they all the money through their factories. We would only be too grateful to be left alone!

SCENE TWO
This scene takes place on April 6,1861, at the Chestnut residence in Charleston, South Carolina.

FIRST NARRATOR: When the Southern states seceded from the Union, they took control of U.S. forts and other government property within their borders. Fort Sumter, however, lying in Charleston Harbor, was still held by U.S. troops. One of Lincoln's first moves as President was to re-supply Fort Sumter with fresh weapons, ammunition, and supplies. James Chestnut, a member of the provisional Confederate government, began to prepare for war.

JAMES CHESTNUT: Lincoln is intent on arming the fort. He's sending in fresh soldiers and supplies. It's clearly an act of war. *(calling)* Laurence! My hat!

MARY CHESTNUT: Certainly Mr. Lincoln will listen to reason.

JAMES CHESTNUT: He hasn't yet. The war council is meeting this evening to decide how to respond.

MARY CHESTNUT: James, do you see any way that war can be avoided?

JAMES CHESTNUT: No, my dear, I don't.

MARY CHESTNUT: Send word to me, James, about what you decide. I had rather know than sit here and wonder.

JAMES CHESTNUT: I will. Laurence!

(He leaves the room.)

SECOND NARRATOR: Maria Whitaker and Laurence are in the kitchen of the Chestnut home.

MARIA WHITAKER: Laurence, Master Jim's calling for his hat. Can't you hear him?

LAURENCE: If it's his hat, then he should be able to find it.

MARIA WHITAKER: What are you talking such nonsense for?

LAURENCE: It's not nonsense, it's the truth.

MARIA WHITAKER: You want to be free, is that it? What would you do? Where would you go?

LAURENCE: You forget—Miss Mary taught me how to read. I guess I can take care of myself all right. Haven't I taken care of Master Jim all these years?

MARIA WHITAKER: I've heard enough. Find the hat and then take Miss Mary her tea.

FIRST NARRATOR: A few minutes later, Laurence takes Mary her tea and sets it down in front of her.

MARY CHESTNUT: Thank you. Laurence, Mr. Lincoln has sent down six men-of-war to sit in our harbor. It appears that we're headed for war.

SECOND NARRATOR: Laurence says nothing and leaves the room. Mary looks puzzled. She rings the bell for Maria. Maria hurries into the room.

MARIA WHITAKER: Yes ma'am?

MARY CHESTNUT: Maria, is anything wrong with Laurence? He's gotten very quiet.

MARIA WHITAKER *(blurting it out):* He should never have learned how to read!

MARY CHESTNUT: Maria! How can you say such a thing?

MARIA WHITAKER: Because now he spends all his time reading the newspapers about Mr. Lincoln and your friend Mr. Davis and the war that's coming, and now his mind is filled with thoughts like things are going to change.

MARY CHESTNUT: Things *are* going to change, Maria, don't you know that? No matter how the war ends, you'll be free. Before we get out of war, we'll have to free you.

MARIA WHITAKER: And then what? Has anybody thought about that?

FIRST NARRATOR: Later that night, Mary wrote again in her diary.

MARY: Not by one word or look can we detect any change in the demeanor of these Negro servants. Laurence sits at the door, as sleepy and as respectful and as profoundly indifferent. So are they all. They carry it too far. You could not tell that they hear anything. And people talk before them as if they were chairs and tables. And they make no sign.

SCENE THREE
This scene takes place the next day—April 7, 1861—in the Chestnuts' parlor.

JULIA TOOMBS: What's going on at the fort? What has James told you? Are we at war yet?

MARY CHESTNUT: Julia. We are not at war.

JULIA TOOMBS: Not yet, Mary. Come now, your husband is the head of the army in South Carolina. I know the war council met last night. He must have some news!

MARY CHESTNUT: I can't think that James knows anything that your husband doesn't. Isn't Mr. Toombs still the Confederacy's Secretary of State?

JULIA TOOMBS: Oh, Mary, you're no fun at all. Don't you think this is the most exciting thing?

MARY CHESTNUT: I've heard enough of this reckless, devil-may-care, headstrong thinking. If we would go to war, then we must prepare for it. We must develop some patience and persistence. We have enough and too much of this pluck and dash.

JULIA TOOMBS: Mary Chestnut, you are nothing but a black ball of gloom today!

MARY CHESTNUT: I want us to be free of the North as much as anyone. What I cannot understand is why they just will not let us go our own way! I cannot understand how our men can believe that all they'll have to do is stand in a line and fire their guns and the Yankees will turn and run away! Don't they know that the North is as convinced that they're right as we're certain that we're right?

JULIA TOOMBS: We *are* right. The North is wrong.

MARY CHESTNUT: This whole disagreement has come about because the South has all the problems of slavery while the North makes all the money off the products of the slaves.

JULIA TOOMBS: Good heavens! What would you have us do? Give up our slaves? Ship them North?

MARY CHESTNUT: Julia Toombs, sometimes you try my patience. Listen to me, the cotton gets milled and where does it go? To the North, to the factories, where it's made into clothes and curtains and bedspreads and sails for ships. When these items are sold, who gets the money? The factory owners in the North. We have to use slaves to pick the cotton that the North needs. Now, don't you think reasonable men can sit around a table and come to an agreement that benefits both sides?

JULIA TOOMBS: It's not just a question of money, Mary. The Constitution says that each state can act in its own right. The North wants to outlaw slavery in the Southern states. They cannot do it. They have no right to do it.

MARY CHESTNUT: Ah, Julia, that stubborn streak may be the undoing of the South.

SCENE FOUR
This scene takes place on April 12, 1861, on the roof of the Chestnuts' house.

FIRST NARRATOR: At midnight, James Chestnut and other Confederate officers rowed out to Fort Sumter. They told Major Robert Anderson that he and his men must surrender the fort by 4:00 A.M. or else the Confederate soldiers would start firing.

SECOND NARRATOR: Mary Chestnut lay in bed and heard a church clock chiming four bells. Thirty minutes later, she heard the sounds of explosions and saw flashes of light from her window. Like almost everyone in Charleston, she rushed up to her roof.

LOUISA HAMILTON: Oh, Mary, isn't it magnificent!

MARY CHESTNUT: It might be if my husband weren't somewhere in a boat in the harbor.

LOUISA HAMILTON: Look! It's only Confederate fire—Fort Sumter's not shooting back! He's perfectly safe. Look how the shells light up the sky! You should hear the baby. He claps his hands and says "Boom! Boom!" every time he hears an explosion.

MARY CHESTNUT: And who knows what death and destruction each one brings? Oh, James, I hope you're safe!

SCENE FIVE
April 15, 1861, in the Chestnuts' parlor.

SECOND NARRATOR: The shelling of Fort Sumter lasted for 34 hours. Then, finally, on April 13, the shelling stopped and the Confederate flag flew over the fort. James Chestnut returned home safely.

JAMES CHESTNUT: Wigfall and I were on Morris Island, waiting to row over to the fort when—

LOUIS WIGFALL: "The fort's on fire!" I shouted and hopped in a boat and rowed right over, waving my white handkerchief like mad, so I wouldn't get shot.

JAMES CHESTNUT: Then he climbed in through a porthole.

LOUIS WIGFALL: You saw that, did you?

 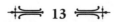

MARY CHESTNUT *(trying not to smile):* Did you have to crawl in through a porthole too, James?

JAMES CHESTNUT: Fortunately, Colonel Anderson received me at the entrance. Very gentlemanly. He did mention that the fort was mined and that we should choose our steps carefully.

MARY CHESTNUT: Mined! And I was worried about all those shells falling on you in the bay!

LOUIS WIGFALL *(jumping up):* I must go! Have to spread the word! Everyone wants to hear about the surrender! And the fort surrendered to me, after all!

(He leaves the room.)

MARY CHESTNUT: Did Major Anderson really surrender to him?

JAMES CHESTNUT: They did indeed. I think the sight of him coming through the porthole scared them more than anything.

MARY CHESTNUT: I don't imagine that all the other battles to come will be as amusing as this one was. Or as victorious. No human lives lost.

JAMES CHESTNUT: Did you know that Major Anderson was Beauregard's teacher at West Point? Can you imagine—Beauregard giving the order to open fire on the man who had taught him how to be a gunner? He gave the American flag to Anderson.

MARY CHESTNUT: There are no clean divisions in this war. If only it were as simple as North and South, or slavery versus freedom.

JAMES CHESTNUT: Old Abe has given us no choice. We've proven that we won't turn away from a fight.

MARY CHESTNUT: Is there no hope at all for negotiation?

JAMES CHESTNUT: None. None at all.

FIRST NARRATOR: That night, Mary wrote in her diary.

MARY CHESTNUT: I did not know one could live through such days of excitement. I am happy James is home, but, we have burned our ships, we are obliged to go on now . .

SECOND NARRATOR: Mary knew that after the fort had surrendered and the Confederate army had taken it over, there would be no turning back. She knew the North would come with an army, and the South would answer in return. She knew the Civil War had begun.

BACKGROUND AND CLASSROOM GUIDE

Background on Mary Chestnut and the Antebellum South

Mary Chestnut was born Mary Boykin in 1825. In 1840, she married James C. Chestnut, Jr. The Boykins and the Chestnuts were among the oldest and wealthiest families in South Carolina.

In many ways Mary's family and her husband's family were typical of the wealthy Southern aristocracy before the war. Each family owned a plantation, and each plantation had hundreds of slaves. The slaves were vital to the successful running of the plantations for the main income was from the cotton fields. Picking cotton is intense, back-breaking work and, in order to be profitable, scores of pickers are needed. If plantation owners had to pay laborers to pick cotton, the argument went, they could not turn a profit.

Strikingly beautiful and fiercely intelligent, Mary Chestnut was popular with her husband's friends and, when he served as United States Senator from South Carolina, she became a favored hostess in Washington, D.C. It was in this way that the Chestnuts became friends with Jefferson Davis and his wife Varina. In her diary, Mary wrote of her curiosity as to what the slaves thought about the war and was also harshly critical of the Confederate government. While she felt slavery was a necessity to the Southern economy, she also wrote of her disgust with how slaves were treated, as well as her feeling that if the slaves were not respected as human beings, they would revolt.

Mary and James Chestnut moved back to South Carolina just before the war when James resigned from the Congress. James later became an advisor to Jefferson Davis as well as an officer in the Confederate army, eventually reaching the rank of brigadier general. When the war ended, the Chestnuts had lost their plantation and were in financial trouble. Mary, crushed by the Southern defeat, stopped writing in her diary around July 1865. Needing money, she tried many times to publish her writings, but her work was not published until twenty years after her death. Mary and James struggled to build a new house, which they finally did in 1873, but by then they were both in poor health. James died in 1885, and Mary died a year later in 1886. She was 63 years old.

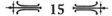

Book Links

Chang, Ina. *A Separate Battle: Women and the Civil War*. New York: Lodestar Books, 1991.

Chestnut, Mary. C. Vann Woodward, ed. *Mary Chestnut's Civil War*. New Haven: Yale University Press, 1981.

Hoobler, Dorothy and Thomas Hoobler. *Sally Bradford: The Story of a Rebel Girl*. Parisppany, NJ: Silver Burdett, 1997.

McKissack, Patricia C. and Frederick L. McKissack. *Christmas in the Big House*. New York: Scholastic, 1994.

Ward, Geoffrey C. *The Civil War: An Illustrated History*. New York: Alfred A. Knopf, 1991.

Classroom Discussion and Activities

DISCUSSION QUESTIONS

• Explain that the vast majority of slaves in the South were illiterate, and discuss how this helped slaveholders maintain control. Ask students who they think would be better prepared for freedom, Maria Whitaker who was illiterate or Laurence who could read? Remind students about Maria's concerns about freedom—where would freed slaves go, what would they do. Have students consider the challenges that would have faced newly freed African Americans in the South. What should the North and the South have done to prepare their societies for the emancipation of the slaves? How could the slaves have prepared themselves for their new lives?

• Mary Chestnut felt that an agreement could be negotiated between the North and the South. Explore the differences between the South and the North with students. Mention the Southern argument that the Northern factory owners made fortunes turning out products made from Southern materials—gathered by slaves—and thus were making as much money off slavery as the South. Also explore other differences between the North and South such as economic (industry versus agriculture), social (urban life versus plantation life), political (slavery as an economic necessity versus slavery as a moral wrong). Use your explorations to try to negotiate an agreement between the North and the South. Split the class equally into Northerners and Southerners. Have students work on an agreement as a class or in groups.

ACTIVITIES

Dear Diary Mary Chestnut's diary shows the real, day-to-day effects of the Civil War. Talk with students about current events in your community, the nation, and the world, and how these events effect their every day lives. Ask each student to choose one current event that they feel is the most important and may have the most relevance to his or her life. Have them keep diaries for at least one month, recording their thoughts and experiences about the event. You may want to read aloud several sections from Mary Chestnut's diary or other Civil War diaries to give students a sense of what they can record including rumors, news reports, conversations among friends, and so on.

Comparing the Confederacy and the United States Governments The Southern states that seceded formed a separate government called the Confederate States of America. Tell students to find out more about the Confederate government—for example, its history, currency, structure, constitution, officials, the states involved, and other details. Then urge them to compare the Confederate government to the United States government. You may assign one topic for comparison to partners or groups of students to research and have them present their findings in creative visual displays to the rest of the class.

Women at War Many women participated in the Civil War directly and indirectly. Nurses, spies, and soldiers such as Clara Barton, Belle Boyd, Harriet Tubman, and Frankie Thompson were in the line of fire. Because most of the Civil War was fought on Southern soil, ordinary Southern women experienced war first hand. While their husbands and sons were fighting, they were in charge of the household duties, which for some, included planting and harvesting crops and managing slaves. Direct students to learn more about the lives of women during the Civil War. Ask each student to focus on one particular woman and write her biography. They may present their work in various forms such as scrapbooks, Web pages, plays, diaries, and so on.

Fire at Fort Sumter The fight for Fort Sumter opened the Civil War. Urge students to research the battle for Fort Sumter. Divide the class into groups of four or five students. Challenge them to create maps to show the progress of the battle. They may also use toy soldiers and boats to represent the action. After they "fight" their battles, ask them to critique the actions of the North and the South. Could the North have successfully held Fort Sumter? Encourage them to draw new flow maps to show their revised strategies for the North and the South.

WHAT THE WAR WAS ABOUT

Frederick Douglass and The Emancipation Proclamation

CAST
(in order of appearance)

First Narrator

Second Narrator

Sarah Carter

Emily Carter } African Americans living in the North

Jessie Carter

Gerrit Smith: Douglass's friend; supporter of the Douglass Monthly

Frederick Douglass: Abolitionist

Salmon P. Chase: United States Secretary of the Treasury

William H. Seward: United States Secretary of State

Edwin Stanton: United States Secretary of War

Abraham Lincoln: Sixteenth president of the United States

SCENE ONE

This scene takes place in April 1861 in a household in Boston, Massachusetts.

FIRST NARRATOR: Frederick Douglass was an abolitionist. Mostly from the Northeast, abolitionists got the name because they worked for the complete abolition, or elimination, of slavery in the United States. They felt their position was morally right, and they refused all compromises. Douglass was one of the strongest voices for abolition. He published his own newspaper *Douglass's Monthly* and in every issue he implored free African Americans living in the North to support Lincoln.

SECOND NARRATOR: With Lincoln's election in 1860, Douglass felt that the time to end slavery was at hand. When the Civil War broke out, Frederick Douglass saw it as a war to end slavery.

FIRST NARRATOR: Abraham Lincoln saw the war as an effort to reunite the United States. He knew he owed his election, in part, to the work of Douglass and the abolitionists. Yet in 1861 with the Civil War raging all around him, he could not afford to have the Border States leave the Union too.

SECOND NARRATOR: The Border States were states on the border of the North and South—Missouri, Maryland, West Virginia, Delaware, and Kentucky—that had chosen to remain with the Union. None of these states, however, had outlawed slavery. If Lincoln stated that the war was a fight against slavery, these states would surely join the Confederacy.

SARAH CARTER (*reading from Douglass's newspaper*): "The last ten days have made a tremendous revolution in all things pertaining to the possible future of the colored people of the United States."

JESSIE CARTER (*reading over Sarah's shoulder*): "We shall stay here and watch the current of events, and serve the cause of humanity in any way that shall be open to us during the struggle now going on between the slave power and the government."

EMILY CARTER (*reading over Sarah's other shoulder*): "Every beat of our heart is with the legitimate American Government, in its determination to suppress and put down this slave-holding rebellion."

SARAH CARTER: Lincoln doesn't want to free any slaves. Hasn't he said that he wouldn't do anything to put an end to slavery in the South?

JESSIE CARTER: He said he'd stop slavery in the territories. You've got to start somewhere. Besides, do you think the South's going to listen to him? They've pulled away from the Union haven't they?

EMILY CARTER: I agree with Frederick Douglass. I'm willing to stay here and watch and serve the cause in any way that I can. Change is coming. There's no doubt about that.

SCENE TWO

This scene takes place in December of 1861 at the offices of the *Douglass Monthly* in Rochester, New York.

FIRST NARRATOR: Douglass's confidence in Lincoln was severely shaken by the president's actions regarding African Americans. For instance, Lincoln upheld the Fugitive Slave Law. This law said that slaves who escaped must be returned to their owners. Union commanders who captured territory in the South often harbored "runaway" slaves. They were commanded by Lincoln to return the fugitives to their owners. Escaping to Washington, D.C., offered no hope to African Americans. They were promptly put into jail until they could be sent back.

SECOND NARRATOR: Frederick Douglass voiced his anger and concern to friends—and in the pages of his newspaper.

GERRIT SMITH: I understand that you're upset, Frederick, but there's a war on.

FREDERICK DOUGLASS: A war being fought over the institution of slavery.

GERRIT SMITH: Tell you what, I'll pretend that I'm Abe Lincoln. You tell me what you'd tell him if you met him face to face. If I were Lincoln, I might tell you something like this *(adjusting his voice):* The war's being fought to keep the country together!

FREDERICK DOUGLASS: If you want to end this war, I can tell you how to end it in a matter of months!

GERRIT SMITH *(pretending to be interested):* Really, Mr. Douglass? And how's that?

FREDERICK DOUGLASS: Stop enforcing the immoral law that requires Union officers to return escaped slaves to their owners in the Slave Power, the South. Allow the men to join the Army—train them, suit them in the uniform of freedom, arm them, and then permit them to go across the lines and fight for their freedom! Let the slaves and freed men be called into service and formed into a liberating army to march into the South and raise the banner of Emancipation among the slaves!

GERRIT SMITH *(politely):* And this will end the war?

FREDERICK DOUGLASS: The simple way to put an end to this savage and desolating war being waged by slaveholders is to strike down slavery itself—the very cause of the war.

GERRIT SMITH: The Southern states caused this war by abandoning the Union. That must be addressed first.

FREDERICK DOUGLASS: Mr. President, when you were in the state legislature in Illinois and, when you were in Congress, you stood up against slavery. You called it—

GERRIT SMITH: the "peculiar institution . . ."

FREDERICK DOUGLASS: The "peculiar institution that deprives men of their God-given freedom." You kept it outlawed in Illinois, and fought for its abolition in the District of Columbia. You kept the disease of slavery from spreading.

GERRIT SMITH: You're quite up on your politics, Mr. Douglass. I have not forgotten my morals, but I am the President of the United States. The entire United States, and that includes the Southern states, no matter what they say or do. Right now the country will not support a war fought over slavery. They *will*, however, support a war to keep the Union together.

FREDERICK DOUGLASS: And where does this leave my people?

GERRIT SMITH: When the war is going better for the Union, and it will, I promise you, I will have the support I need to do what I need to do. Give me some time, Mr. Douglass. I will not forget you.

FREDERICK DOUGLASS: We've waited hundreds of years for our freedom, Mr. President. I don' t know how much longer we can wait.

GERRIT SMITH *(dropping his role as Abraham Lincoln):* Tell the President what you've just told me. Tell the people of the North and the South.

SCENE THREE
This scene takes place in July of 1862 in Boston and in Washington, D.C.

FIRST NARRATOR: Douglass did just that. His words reached ordinary households—

SARAH CARTER *(reading from the newspaper):* "Notwithstanding the Presidents' repeated declarations that he considers slavery an evil, every step of his Presidential career relating to slavery proves him active, decided, and brave for its support and passive, cowardly, and treacherous to the very cause of liberty to which he owes his election."

EMILY CARTER *(reading over Sarah's shoulder):* "Some think it is even now too late. We have bowed so low to the dark and bloody spirit of slavery, that it is doubted whether we have the needed moral stamina to save our country from destruction, whether we shall give up the contest, patch up a deceitful peace and restore the slave power to more than its former power and influence in the republic."

JESSIE CARTER *(reading over Sarah's other shoulder):* "Nevertheless, we have strong grounds for hope. The rebels are firm, determined, enthusiastic, and wonderfully successful. The South will not listen to any compromise, and we hope this will compel the Federal Government to at last take *the* step, to destroy the slaveholders by destroying slavery itself. Slavery must die if the nation lives, and the nation must die if slavery lives."

SECOND NARRATOR: And Douglass's words reached the White House—

SALMON P. CHASE: There's quite a call in the North for freeing the slaves.

WILLIAM H. SEWARD: I'm an abolitionist, Chase, but even I say that it can't be done. Not right now. You know that.

SALMON P. CHASE: We have a moral obligation—

WILLIAM H. SEWARD: We have a moral obligation to win the war and keep the nation together. If we lose, then slavery will never be outlawed. Need I remind you that our army is not winning right now? We've lost at Bull Run. The Peninsular Campaign failed to capture Richmond, and we don't seem to have a general who can keep Robert E. Lee from making us look stupid.

ABRAHAM LINCOLN: Gentlemen, I have thought long and hard over this question. Until recently, I believed that we would be able to end the war and bring the South back into the Union. Now I believe that only a total victory on our side will ensure that. We can win only if we outlaw slavery there. It is the labor of black men and women—gunsmiths and nurses and field hands—that fuels Southern armies. I'm giving the South until January 1 of next year to return to the Union. If not, then their slaves shall be then and forever free.

WILLIAM H. SEWARD: Mr. President, you cannot issue a proclamation like that. The time isn't right. We must at least *seem* to be winning the war when you emancipate the slaves.

ABRAHAM LINCOLN: I understand your concerns, Mr. Seward. I share them, but the time will soon be right. I must begin to prepare the people for an emancipation proclamation.

SCENE FOUR
This scene takes place on September 22, 1862, at the White House in Washington, D.C.

FIRST NARRATOR: In September of 1862, Lee led his Confederate troops across the Potomac River and into Maryland. A complete set of Lee's battle plans was found at an abandoned Confederate camp by a Union soldier. Thanks to this discovery, the Union commander, General George McClellan found Lee and his army at Sharpsburg, Maryland, between the Potomac River and Antietam Creek.

SECOND NARRATOR: Although losses on both sides were high and nearly equal, McClellan had a reserve force of 20,000 men. These men probably could have destroyed Lee's army. Instead, the Confederates were able to retreat across the Potomac.

ABRAHAM LINCOLN: Gentlemen, what news?

EDWIN M. STANTON: Our army has met Lee's forces at Antietam Creek in Maryland.

ABRAHAM LINCOLN: And?

EDWIN M. STANTON: General McClellan's men suffered about 12,000 casualties, including over 2,000 dead. Lee has had about the same number of casualties, and he was forced to pull his men back across the creek.

WILLIAM H. SEWARD: It's a draw. A tie. Our side kills the same number of men that their side kills.

ABRAHAM LINCOLN: You say that McClellan pushed Lee back?

EDWIN M. STANTON: That's the report.

ABRAHAM LINCOLN: The enemy retreated. That's not a draw, it's a win for our side.

EDWIN M. STANTON: A slim one at best.

ABRAHAM LINCOLN: Forcing the enemy to retreat is a victory. That's exactly what we need right now. Mr. Seward, I want you to contact your friends at the newspapers. Twist their arms and convince them to write stories about our glorious victory at the Battle of Antietam.

EDWIN M. STANTON: I would hardly call this a glorious victory. We barely managed to get out of there with our army intact.

ABRAHAM LINCOLN: I made a vow before this battle, gentlemen. I swore that I would take a victory at Antietam as a sign from God that I should issue the Emancipation Proclamation. I have received a sign. Tomorrow, alongside the news of our victory at Antietam, the newspapers will carry the proclamation. The South shall have its warning.

SCENE FIVE

This scene takes place in July of 1863 at the White House in Washington, D.C.

FIRST NARRATOR: President Lincoln signed the Emancipation Proclamation on January 1, 1863. The proclamation freed all the slaves in the Southern states and allowed African American soldiers to join the Union army.

SECOND NARRATOR: In his newspaper, Frederick Douglass rejoiced. *(reading from Douglass's newspaper)* "Common sense, the necessities of war, to say nothing of the dictation of justice and humanity have at last prevailed. We shout for joy that we live to record this righteous decree! Abraham Lincoln, President of the United States, Commander-in-Chief of the army and navy, in his own peculiar cautious, forbearing and hesitating way, slow, but we hope sure, has, while the loyal heart was near breaking with despair, proclaimed and declared: That on the First of January, in the Year of Our Lord 1863, all persons held as slaves within any state or any designated part of a state, the people whereof shall then be in rebellion against the United States, shall be then, thenceforward, and forever free! Free forever! Oh, long enslaved millions! Whose cries have so vexed the air and sky, the hour of your deliverance has come! Lift up now your voices with joy and thanksgiving for with freedom to the slaves will come peace and safety to your country!"

FIRST NARRATOR: Soon after the Emancipation Proclamation was signed, Lincoln and Douglass met. Since the proclamation, Douglass had been working hard to recruit African American soldiers. He soon realized, however, that black soldiers were not being treated well. Douglass met with Lincoln face-to-face to voice his concerns.

FREDERICK DOUGLASS: Mr. President, I am Frederick—

ABRAHAM LINCOLN *(smiling and extending his hand):* I know who you are, Mr. Douglass. I'm glad to see you. Please, sit down.

FREDERICK DOUGLASS: Sir, I applaud you for issuing the Emancipation Proclamation.

ABRAHAM LINCOLN: Thank you, Mr. Douglass. And thank you for your gentle reminders of what is right and what is important. The country owes you a debt for that.

FREDERICK DOUGLASS: On the contrary, the country owes a debt to its black soldiers. They must receive equal pay and an equal chance for promotion as white soldiers. Their lives are no less valuable. You must guarantee to retaliate for any black soldiers captured during battle who are then mistreated or killed.

ABRAHAM LINCOLN: I fear that I'm about to disappoint you again, Mr. Douglass. I cannot promise equal pay for black soldiers. The public will not, as yet, support that. I can promise, though, that in the end, they shall have the same pay as white soldiers. As for promotions, I will sign any recommendations concerning black soldiers that the Secretary of War sends me. *(Lincoln is quiet for a moment.)* The abuse and murder of black soldiers disturbs me greatly, but again, I cannot promise to retaliate.

FREDERICK DOUGLASS: I appreciate your honesty, Mr. President. You've given me less than I had hoped for, but I won't give up. You'll be hearing from me soon.

ABRAHAM LINCOLN: I look forward to that.

(Both men rise and shake hands. Douglass is about to the leave the office when Lincoln's voice stops him.)

ABRAHAM LINCOLN: Mr. Douglass—it appears, after all, that you now have your wish. The war is about slavery now.

FREDERICK DOUGLASS: It always was, Mr. President. It always was.

BACKGROUND AND CLASSROOM GUIDE

Background on Frederick Douglass

Born Frederick Augustus Washington Bailey on February 7, 1817, Frederick Douglass grew up as a slave in Maryland. As a boy, he witnessed the harsh treatment of his father, which instilled in him a hatred of slavery. Frederick attempted one unsuccessful escape in 1836, and finally, with the help of the Underground Railroad—the network of freed slaves and abolitionists—Douglass did escape to Massachusetts in 1838. Calling himself a "recent graduate from the institution of slavery with my diploma on my back," Douglass began his career as an abolitionist and orator. Traveling around the North, he gave speeches decrying the evils of slavery and telling of the horrors of life as a slave that helped the Abolitionist movement grow in strength and number. In fact, Douglass was such a good orator and writer that people began to doubt that he had been a slave, claiming he was a well-educated impostor propped up by abolitionists. In response, Douglass published his autobiography in 1854 called *Narrative of the Life of Frederick Douglass, an American Slave,* proving he was as good a writer as a speaker.

Douglass took up residence in Rochester, New York, and from there published his own newspaper *Douglass's Monthly.* As Abraham Lincoln rose to prominence, Douglass campaigned for him to be elected President. Douglass knew Lincoln believed slavery to be a moral wrong, but upon Lincoln's election, he grew impatient with the President for not immediately granting the southern slaves their freedom. Lincoln, who felt hampered by the possible political implications of such a move early in the war, waited for a Union battlefield victory before finally issuing the Emancipation Proclamation in 1863.

Douglas firmly believed that the way to end the Civil War quickly was to raise an army of black men, including freed slaves, and use that army to invade the South. He went so far as to impress upon Lincoln himself the importance of such a move, and soon after the outbreak of the war raised two regiments of black soldiers, both of which fought with bravery and distinction in the Civil War.

Douglass fought for the enactment of the 13th, 14th, and 15th Amendments after the Civil War, the so-called Civil Rights amendments that respectively outlawed slavery, guaranteed that no state could take away a person's rights, and gave the vote to African American men. He later became United States Minister to Haiti. Douglass died in Washington, D.C. on February 20, 1895. He was 78 years old.

Book Links

Cox, Clinton. *Undying Glory: The Story of the Massachusetts Fifty-Fourth Regiment.*
New York: Scholastic, 1993.

Douglass, Frederick. *Escape from Slavery: The Boyhood of Frederick Douglass in His Own Words.* New York: Knopf, 1994.

Marrin, Albert. *Commander in Chief: Abraham Lincoln and the Civil War.* New York: Dutton Children's Books, 1997.

Miller, Douglas T. *Frederick Douglass and the Fight for Freedom.* New York: Facts on File Publications, 1988.

Paulsen, Gary. *Nightjohn.* New York: Delacorte, 1993.

Classroom Discussion and Activities

DISCUSSION QUESTIONS

• At the end of the play, Lincoln says to Douglass, "The war is about slavery, now." Douglass replies, "It always was, Mr. President, it always was." Discuss with students what each man meant. Review why President Lincoln waited as long as he did before issuing the Emancipation Proclamation, and list his reasons on the board. Ask students if they agree or disagree with Lincoln's actions. Did he realize that the war was always about slavery, or was it about keeping the Union together? Was Douglass right in his thinking that all the reasons for fighting were rooted in the South's practice of slavery?

• Douglass once said that his mission was to "agitate, agitate, agitate." Ask students to define the word "agitate" in the way that Douglass used it. Do they feel there is a time and a place for this type of action? Have them identify issues that they feel are worth agitating for today. How do they compare these issues with Frederick Douglass and his struggle to end slavery? To extend the discussion, encourage groups of students who share concerns over the same issues to publish their own newsletters like the Douglass Monthly.

ACTIVITIES

Time for a Change The election of Abraham Lincoln caused major changes in the United States. Have students chart these changes on a timeline. Ask them to begin the timeline in November 1860 when Lincoln was elected. Assign the time periods covered in the plays to different groups of students. Give each group a section of chart paper that corresponds to its time period; each year should appear on the timeline. They should conduct additional research to find out other important Civil War events that were occurring at the same time. Urge students to be creative and to include text as well as illustrations on their timelines.

The Border States Remind students that the border states of Maryland, Missouri, Delaware, Kentucky, and West Virginia were strategically and politically important to the North. It was said of these states that "Lincoln would like to have God on his side, but he must have Kentucky." Challenge students to consider why Kentucky and the other states were so important to Lincoln and the North. Divide the class into five groups—one for each Border State. Tell them to study United States maps and determine the strategic importance of the Border States to the North—and to the South. Ask them to create their own maps showing important Northern and Southern cities, important physical features such as the Mississippi River, flow lines to indicate possible advances of Northern and/or Southern troops, and so on.

Who Were the Abolitionists? Frederick Douglass, Angelina and Sarah Grimké, John Brown, and William Lloyd Garrison were influential abolitionists before and during the Civil War. Have each student research the life of a famous abolitionist. What led each person to focus his or her energies on the freedom of African Americans? How did each person's background—family, childhood, environment—contribute to him or her becoming an abolitionist? As a class, discuss the similarities and differences among the abolitionists. Based on their research, can students draw conclusions about the abolitionists?

Roles of African Americans Before and During the Civil War The Emancipation Proclamation called for the freedom of the Southern slaves and for the mustering of black soldiers and sailors. How did the Proclamation change the lives of African Americans in the North and in the South? Direct students to find out more about the history of slavery in the United States; African American soldiers (both Union and Confederate); and the lives of enslaved black men, women, and children during the Civil War. Guide students to examine a variety of primary sources such as diaries, slave narratives, and Frederick Douglass's writings to understand what life was like for African Americans before and during the Civil War.

THE TURNING POINT

The Battle of Gettysburg

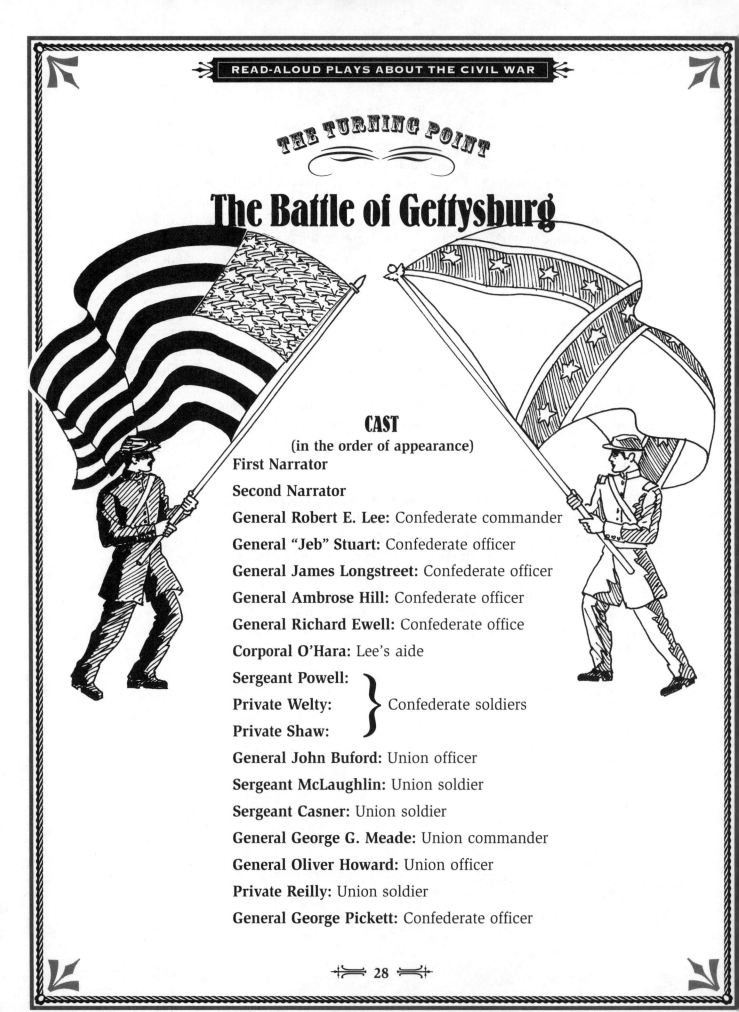

CAST

(in the order of appearance)

First Narrator

Second Narrator

General Robert E. Lee: Confederate commander

General "Jeb" Stuart: Confederate officer

General James Longstreet: Confederate officer

General Ambrose Hill: Confederate officer

General Richard Ewell: Confederate office

Corporal O'Hara: Lee's aide

Sergeant Powell: ⎫
Private Welty: ⎬ Confederate soldiers
Private Shaw: ⎭

General John Buford: Union officer

Sergeant McLaughlin: Union soldier

Sergeant Casner: Union soldier

General George G. Meade: Union commander

General Oliver Howard: Union officer

Private Reilly: Union soldier

General George Pickett: Confederate officer

SCENE ONE

This scene takes place in the summer of 1863 in Virginia at General Lee's headquarters.

FIRST NARRATOR: The Civil War has been, up to this point, successful for the Confederate Army under the command of General Robert E. Lee. In early May, they won the Battle of Chancellorsville.

SECOND NARRATOR: But General Lee knew that his army, though larger and stronger than it had been, could not hold out against the better-supplied Union troops. He knew he had to use the advantage he had to try to bring the war to a quick end.

LEE: Generals, with 75,000 men, our army right now nearly equals the Union army. The Yankees are disorganized from the defeat of Chancellorsville. We have momentum. The time has come for a bold move—an invasion of the North.

STUART: It's about time! Strike them in their very heart!

LONGSTREET: We have the advantage when we fight on our own territory. I don't much fancy fighting the enemy on his own turf.

HILL: We'll be vastly outnumbered—

EWELL: We tried this once before—at Antietam—and we suffered terrible losses. Why take the risk?

LEE: For Several reasons. First, our farmland and crops have been destroyed by the war. Northern farms have been spared. We need their supplies. Then there's the matter of General Hooker. When he sees that we're moving north, he'll hurry to guard Washington. If nothing else, I've learned that most Northern generals prefer to defend than to attack. While he guards the capital, we'll have our sights on Philadelphia and Baltimore. I want to sever Washington from the rest of the country. Finally, when the Yankees see that we can invade them, they'll be ready to negotiate an end to this war. We can ask for peace from a position of strength.

HILL: It may be the only way to shock some sense into the Yankees.

EWELL: I doubt that we would meet any opposition from Hooker.

LONGSTREET (*stubbornly*): I'm not convinced. It's a long march. We're winning now. Let's use that advantage to raise more troops and defend our borders.

LEE: We have no more troops to raise. Our army is as strong as it will ever be. We can defend our borders until all our men are dead or captured—and then we'll have no more borders. If we move now, we catch our enemy by surprise. If we invade their territory, we take the fight to them. They'll have no energy for that. With our army standing on their land, they'll look at the conflict, and us, in a new light.

HILL: Confederate troops standing on Yankee soil. I like the sound of that.

LONGSTREET: Do you like the sound of Union soldiers swarming over our borders and taking us in chains to Washington?

EWELL: That's not going to happen.

LEE: Are we agreed?

HILL, EWELL, AND STUART: Yes!

LONGSTREET: It appears that I'm outvoted. *(reluctantly)* We march.

LEE: Good. General Stuart, I want you and the cavalry to engage the Union troops as much as possible. If you keep them busy, we'll be able to slip into Pennsylvania without notice. More importantly, I want you to find out how strong they are and where they are. I'll expect you to join us in Pennsylvania in a few days. It's vital that we know the strength and location of the Union army as quickly as possible. Understood?

STUART: You can count on me, sir! I'll ride circles around Hooker and his troops!

LEE: Just do what I ask, Jeb. No more and no less.

SCENE TWO
This scene takes place on June 28, 1863, inside Lee's tent at Martinsburg, Pennsylvania.

FIRST NARRATOR: General Lee's plan began to fall apart quickly. He was in his tent after a hard day of marching from Virginia through Maryland into Pennsylvania, expecting to hear news from Jeb Stuart. The news came from a different source.

O'HARA: General Lee! General Lee! I have news from General Jackson back in Virginia!

LEE: At last, some word on the enemy. Believe me, Corporal, when things in a war get too quiet, it's never good. Open the letter and tell me what General Jackson says.

O'HARA: Word has reached Virginia that General Hooker has been replaced as commander of the Federal Army by General George Meade.

LEE: Meade! I knew both Hooker and Meade at West Point. Meade is twice as smart and three times as tough.

O'HARA: There's more, sir. The Yankees have left Virginia. They're moving north. Sir . . . they're about thirty-five miles away from us.

LEE: So now they're following *us*. That's Meade, all right. I'm surprised he was able to organize himself and his command that fast. No matter. He won't be ready for a fight yet. We need to move faster. We need to keep the Yankees following us, not the other way around. Gather the generals. Tell them I want to continue the march into Pennsylvania at first light.

O'HARA: Yes, sir!

SCENE THREE
This scene takes place on June 30, 1863, at Gettysburg, Pennsylvania.

SECOND NARRATOR: Upon learning that Meade was taking his army North as well, Lee decided to concentrate his entire force at the little town of Gettysburg, just over the Pennsylvania/Maryland border. Meade, however, had figured out Lee's plan and moved to cut off the Confederate Army.

FIRST NARRATOR: Meanwhile the Confederate army, exhausted from the march, was in need of rest and supplies. A patrol from General Ewell's infantry corps went into Gettysburg to see what it could scare up. At the same time, Major General John Buford, under orders to locate the Confederate soldiers and report back to Meade, was leading his men up Cemetery Hill outside of Gettysburg. The hill gave Buford a view of the countryside—countryside filled with gray uniforms.

POWELL: Hey! Y'all find anything?

WELTY: Nothing. Yankees heard we were coming, shut their doors, their stores, their windows.

SHAW: Dang! Where would you hide if you were a storehouse filled with shoes?

WELTY: Shoes?

SHAW: Shoes. Men's shoes.

WELTY: Shoes! Don't talk to me about shoes. My feet are so wet and sore from these old worn boots that I've been thinking about marching on my hands.

POWELL: Remember—we have orders not to provoke the locals.

WELTY: I'm not going to provoke the locals. I'm just going to get me some shoes.

SHAW: Hold up! Look at the foot of that hill yonder! Blue coats! *(He raises his rifle and fires, but the Union soldiers are too far away.)* Dang!

POWELL: Shaw—find General Ewell—*fast!* Tell him we've spotted the enemy!

SECOND NARRATOR: The Confederate patrol retreated. Buford stayed where he was and sent a message back to Meade.

BUFORD: Mac! Tell General Meade that we've found the Confederate army at Gettysburg.

McLAUGHLIN: Yes, sir.

BUFORD: Reilly! Take your men into town. Hold it, and keep the roads clear. You hear me? Casner! Spread the word—I want the men to hunker down on the ridge. Tell them to dig in deep. Mac! Come back here! Tell the general that we hold the town and the roads, and that we'll hold Lee's army back until reinforcements arrive. Hurry!

CASNER: At least we've got the high ground ahead of Lee, but we're only 2,500 strong. These small cannons won't stop a Confederate attack for long, and you know that Lee will throw everything at us.

BUFORD: Reinforcements will be here by morning. Besides, didn't 3,000 of us hold off 25,000 rebels for over six hours in Virginia? We're on our own territory now. We have the advantage. Make sure the men are settled in and ready to fight.

SCENE FOUR
This scene takes place on July 1, 1863, at Gettysburg, Pennsylvania.

FIRST NARRATOR: General Hill's Confederate advance brigades met General Howard's Union cavalry division in a field outside of Gettysburg. Although Hill only had an advance brigade, which is lightly armed and small in manpower, his men fought hard and held the line against Howard's Union troops.

SECOND NARRATOR: Just as Hill's men were about to give out, General Ewell arrived with his troops to join the battle.

FIRST NARRATOR: With the reinforcements, the Confederates pushed the Union troops back across the field and away from the town. Howard's men retreated to the hills outside of Gettysburg—Cemetery Ridge, Cemetery Hill, and Culp's Hill.

SECOND NARRATOR: That night, General Howard reported on the day's battle to Meade.

MEADE: How bad is it?

HOWARD: Our losses were greater than theirs, sir. Over 4,000 of our men were taken prisoner. Lee must have about 70,000 men, and each one of them is fighting like a demon. Should we retreat?

MEADE: No. No retreat. If we do, Lee will drive further north. Eventually he'll march all the way through Pennsylvania and into the capital. No, we have to hold him here. We have no alternative.

HOWARD: What are your orders?

MEADE: We still outnumber them. If we make our line of attack long and curved, then Lee will have to stretch out his men along it. His army will be thin all along that line. We'll hold our ground until his men give out, then we'll move in, and surround him.

HOWARD: It just might work.

MEADE: It has to work.

FIRST NARRATOR: At the same time, several miles away, Lee was taking stock of the situation.

LEE: Tomorrow we attack both flanks of the Union line. General Longstreet, you'll attack the left flank. At the same time, Ewell will attack the right flank at Culp's Hill. I want the Union Army off the high ground and on the run.

LONGSTREET: With all respect, sir, I suggest that we go around them and attack from the rear.

LEE: Stuart's not back yet. We still don't know where all of the Union troops are, or how many there are. Without that information, we run the risk of being ambushed if we circle them.

LONGSTREET: We can't wait on Jeb Stuart! We have to take the chance now and attack Meade from the rear. It's the only way!

LEE: I won't send my men into an ambush. Don't fight me on this.

LONGSTREET: I'm not your enemy, sir. I'm with you, all the way.

SCENE FIVE
This scene takes place on July 2, 1863, at Gettysburg, Pennsylvania.

SECOND NARRATOR: The next day Meade ordered his army to hold their horseshoe position on the Gettysburg hills. His men were curved around Cemetery Ridge, Culp's Hill, Round Top, and Little Round Top. Lee deployed his troops in a long thin line, with Longstreet and Ewell at either end and Hill in the center.

FIRST NARRATOR: Lee's army attacked the right and left flanks of the Union army. The Confederate infantry searched for and attacked weak spots in the middle of the Union line. Soon, smoke from the cannons on both sides clouded the battlefield. From their position, Meade and Howard watched the action.

HOWARD: Longstreet is charging our left flank—I can't tell who's charging our right. There's Lee in the middle!

MEADE: We'll hold them.

HOWARD: Look at that! They're charging right into our cannons with swords and rifles! They just keep coming, stepping over the bodies of their brothers!

MEADE: Keep firing. Hold the line.

HOWARD: General—they're outgunned! They're getting massacred—won't those rebels ever give up?

MEADE: If we hold the line, they will. Lee wants to win, but he's not crazy.

SECOND NARRATOR: By the end of the day, Lee's army had taken parts of Culp's Hill, but Meade's men still held Cemetery Ridge, Round Top, and Little Round Top. Lee's army lost 1,500 men that day.

FIRST NARRATOR: That night Meade held a council of war with his generals.

MEADE: Generals, your thoughts?

HOWARD: Lee's men fight to the death. If we continue, our losses will be tremendous.

MEADE: We still have an advantage in men and guns. If we hold, I don't think Lee has more than one day of fight left in him.

HOWARD: I disagree. We know from prior battles how determined Lee and his army are. He could pull his men back into the woods and hide there until reinforcements arrive. We could fight tomorrow, take heavy losses, and find ourselves right back here in a month or so.

MEADE: Why do you think Lee would charge into a line where he was so outnumbered?

HOWARD: He thought he could push us back.

MEADE: No. If help were coming, Lee would have held his position. This is all he has. This is where it stops. If we pull back, he'll have the time he needs to regroup. There'll be no retreat. We fight tomorrow.

HOWARD: It will be brutal.

MEADE: That's the nature of war. We didn't start this, but if we have a chance to finish it, then we have to do it.

SCENE SIX

This scene takes place on July 3, 1863, at Gettysburg, Pennsylvania.

SECOND NARRATOR: On July 3, the Union soldiers were secure in their positions, while the Confederates had fallen back into the woods surrounding the field. With his men and supplies dwindling, Lee decided to put all his men in one spot to try to break though the middle of the Union line. On Cemetery Ridge, the Union soldiers watched and waited.

McLAUGHLIN: Where are they, Sarge?

REILLY: They're out there, Private, don't you worry.

CASNER: It's almost noon. Aren't they ever going to attack?

McLAUGHLIN: Maybe they changed their minds and went home.

REILLY: They're out there in the woods, probably looking over our line and trying to find the place to focus their attack. If they wait, they think they may catch us off guard. Stay alert men.

CASNER: Sarge! There—by that clump of trees!

REILLY: Prepare your weapons, men! What did you see, Casner?

CASNER: Straight ahead . . . a glint—

FIRST NARRATOR: Gunshot exploded from the woods.

McLAUGHLIN: I'm hit! I'm hit!

CASNER: Sarge!

REILLY: Mac, are you all right?

CASNER: Sarge! Look! It's the whole Reb army! Coming out of the woods!

REILLY: Pull back! Pull back! Mac, are you all right? Mac! MAC!

SECOND NARRATOR: Confederate General George Pickett charged up Cemetery Ridge. Pickett and his men were to charge under the cover of Confederate cannons. The order to charge was delayed. The Confederate officer in charge of artillery twice urged Pickett to attack quickly or risk running out of cannon fire. Unwilling to give the order himself, Longstreet had passed the task to someone else. Pickett wanted to hear the order from Longstreet who was his superior officer. When Longstreet refused to say anything, Pickett began the charge. It was successful at first, but then. . .

POWELL: Charge! Charge!

WELTY: We're being beaten to a pulp!

SHAW: You keep charging or *I'll* shoot you!

WELTY: But it's hopeless!

SHAW: If we retreat now, we'll lose the battle. If we lose this battle, we'll lost the war. If we lose the war, we lose everything!

POWELL: He's right, Private. Charge!

SHAW AND WELTY: Charge!

SECOND NARRATOR: The attack on July 3 became known as Pickett's Charge. And while Lee's men fought with incredible bravery, they marched into certain doom. They attacked the Union line head-on, a line that bombarded them with rifle and cannon fire. Pickett's men broke the first line of the Union defense, but when there weren't enough soldiers to follow them in, Meade's army turned and held.

FIRST NARRATOR: When Pickett finally ordered the retreat, three out of every four men on the Confederate side were lost, including Sergeant Powell, and Privates Welty and Shaw. At his base, Lee ordered the retreat of his army back into Virginia.

LEE: I want every wounded man who can't walk loaded on a wagon. Tell everyone to be ready. Meade knows how decimated we are. He'll no doubt follow us right back into Virginia.

LONGSTREET: Maybe not. His men are as exhausted as ours are. They won't be running for their lives.

LEE: This was all my fault, Longstreet. Let's do the best we can toward saving those we have left.

SECOND NARRATOR: There was no celebrating in Meade's camp, either.

HOWARD: The line held on Cemetery Ridge, General. Lee's retreating. He's probably heading back to Virginia.

MEADE: And our losses?

HOWARD: About three thousand killed, 14,000 wounded, and 5,000 taken as prisoners. Should we organize the troops to follow Lee?

MEADE: No.

HOWARD *(surprised):* No?

MEADE: No.

HOWARD: But if we follow Lee to Virginia, we can destroy his army! We might even be able to take Richmond!

MEADE: It would take months to do that. Look at the men. We have fought, and now we have to bury the dead before we fight again. It's been three days of nonstop death. That's enough for now.

FIRST NARRATOR: Some say Meade's decision not to chase Lee made the war last longer because it gave Lee the opportunity to go back to Virginia, regroup, and fight for almost two more years.

SECOND NARRATOR: The toll at the Battle of Gettysburg was extremely high. Meade's army lost 3,000 men; 15,000 were wounded; and 5,500 were taken prisoner. Lee's losses were higher: He lost 3,500 men; 18,000 were wounded; and 5,000 were taken prisoner. A cemetery was built on the site of the battle where so many men from both sides had fallen. President Lincoln dedicated the cemetery, and the speech he gave, which explained why so many men had died, has gone down in history as the Gettysburg Address.

BACKGROUND AND CLASSROOM GUIDE

Background on the Battle of Gettysburg

By 1863, against all odds, the Confederate Army appeared to be winning the War Between the States. Under the command of Robert E. Lee, the Army of Northern Virginia had defeated the Union army at the battles of Bull Run, the Battle of the Seven Days, and the Battles of Fredericksburg and Chancellorsville. Lee, knowing his troops' morale was high but supplies were low, decided to take the bold move of invading Pennsylvania in the hopes of bringing the war to a quick end and suing for a peace that would be satisfactory to the South. He calculated that he could overcome his disadvantages in numbers by surprising the Union army with the invasion and also taking advantage of its weak leadership. Not discouraged by the disastrous attempt at Antietam to bring his army into Northern territory, Lee moved out.

After learning that General George G. Meade had replaced Joseph "Fighting Joe" Hooker as Union commander and that Meade was leading his army north, Lee decided to focus on the town of Gettysburg, whose high ground and location near the Maryland border made it strategically important. Thinking he had some days before Meade caught up with him, Lee set about establishing a base of operations at Gettysburg. When a patrol of Confederate troops, looking for supplies, encountered Union cavalry in the town, Lee knew that Meade was there.

The battle began on July 1 with fierce fighting on both sides. The Union troops held the ground atop the hills including Round Top, Little Round Top, and Cemetery Ridge. Out-manned and outgunned, Lee's men tried many charges into the Union line, only to be met with blistering cannon fire. The Confederates fought fiercely, and by the night of July 2, the Union army was considering retreating. Unwilling to give up the high ground, Meade ordered that the Union line be fortified.

Lee, thinking the Union line was softening, ordered a last charge on July 3. After firing what was left of his artillery into the Union line, General George Pickett charged up Cemetery Ridge. The charge failed, and over 1,000 Confederate soldiers died on the hill. Lee was left with no choice but to retreat.

When Lee pulled back, he ordered his army back to Virginia, certain Meade would follow his crippled forces. Meade, however, did not follow. Historians have advanced many theories as to why Meade did not seek to deliver what could have been the death blow to the Confederate Army. Some say that he and his army were weary from the battle; some say the heavy rains that fell in the area after July 3 would have made movement difficult. Still

others think that Meade was being merciful after the bloody battle in which nearly 8,000 men on both sides lost their lives. Whatever the reason, Meade's decision not to follow Lee angered Lincoln, and was one reason Meade was replaced by General Ulysses Grant soon after.

Book Links

Collier, James Lincoln and Christopher Collier. *With Every Drop of Blood: A Novel of the Civil War.* New York: Laurel Leaf, 1997.

Crane, Stephen. *The Red Badge of Courage.* New York: Puffin Books, 1995.

Fleischman, Paul. *Bull Run.* New York: Harper Trophy, 1995.

Murphy, Jim. *The Long Road to Gettysburg.* New York: Clarion Books, 1992.

Classroom Discussion and Activities

DISCUSSION QUESTIONS

• Explore issues of bravery and of war. Encourage students to list common acts of bravery and selflessness they see every day. Then discuss whether they feel war is ever right. Do they think the generals on both sides of the battle of Gettysburg made the right decisions, even though thousands of men died on the battlefield? What would have been the consequences if either side had decided not to fight? Would that have been a brave decision? What effect might that have had on the war?

• The people of Gettysburg, with the help of governors from 18 Northern states, bought land for a National Soldiers' Cemetery at the site of the battlefield. President Lincoln received an invitation to the dedication ceremony, but no one expected him to attend, much less deliver a speech. The main speaker, Edward Everett, held the stage for over two hours before Lincoln spoke. In contrast, the President's speech lasted about two minutes. Some newspapers branded the speech as "dull," "silly," and "vulgar." Other newspapers said the speech must be read to be appreciated. Distribute copies of Lincoln's Gettysburg Address to each student, or write the speech on the board and have students copy it. Tell half of the class to read the speech silently to themselves at home, and the other half to read aloud the speech at home. Ask them to read the speech slowly and carefully and to think about why it was written. The next day discuss with students their feelings about the speech. What conclusions did they draw from their readings—is the speech better read or delivered?

ACTIVITIES

Pictures of War The Civil War was the first American war to be photographed. Photographers such as Matthew Brady, Tim O'Sullivan, Alexander Gardner, and G.G. Walker showed Americans citizens what war was like. Challenge students to find a variety of photographs of the Civil War in books, magazines, and the Internet. Have students select several pictures that make the greatest impression on them. Then ask them to write descriptions of what the pictures tell them about war. Emphasize that you're looking for their personal responses.

Historical Hindsight Historians analyze events such as the Battle of Gettysburg and examine such questions as: Was Lee right to invade the North? Should Meade have followed him? Should Lee have waited for more supplies to arrive before crossing the border into Pennsylvania? Have students choose one of these questions or formulate their own, and then research and write reports based on their findings.

The Turning Point? Remind students that Gettysburg is often considered to be the turning point of the Civil War. Challenge them to study the major battles of the Civil War and compare each against the Battle of Gettysburg. How would they rank the battle in terms of importance, and why? Some students may want to extend their research into a study of the battle itself; for example, the role that geography played (the natural defenses that the hills outside Gettysburg offered); a detailed re-enactment of the three-day battle using models; or a story map showing Lee's advance into the North and his eventual retreat to Virginia.

Lincoln and Pickett Many connections existed between the leaders of the Union and Confederate armies. Officers on both sides—including Lee, Hooker, Longstreet, and Meade—attended West Point together. James Longstreet was a friend of Ulysses S. Grant's and attended Grant's wedding. In another peculiar twist of fate, Abraham Lincoln was responsible for helping George Pickett get into West Point. Pickett, a lawyer who wanted a military career, met Lincoln in Illinois when Lincoln was a member of Congress. After the South surrendered and Richmond was occupied by Federal troops, Lincoln visited George Pickett's house. Pickett was not at home, but his wife entertained the President. Have students conduct further research on the relationship between Abraham Lincoln and George Pickett, and then write a play dramatizing their friendship. They may also choose to write plays based on other friendships severed by the Civil War.

SURRENDER AT APPOMATTOX

General Grant and General Lee Meet Again

ROBERT E. LEE

ULYSSES S. GRANT

CAST
(in order of appearance)

First Narrator

Second Narrator

Abraham Lincoln: Sixteenth President of the United States

General Ulysses S. Grant: Commander of the Union Army

General Robert E. Lee: Commander of the Confederate Army

General James Longstreet: Confederate general

General John B. Gordon: Confederate general

General Henry A. Wise: Confederate general

General George G. Meade: Union general

Vincent: General Meade's aide

Captain Nash: Confederate officer

General Philip Sheridan: Union general

SCENE ONE

This scene takes place in February 1864 at the White House in Washington, D.C.

FIRST NARRATOR: The war continued to drag on. The year 1864 is an election year. The voters will soon decide whether to keep Abraham Lincoln in office. During the course of the war, Lincoln had had to push his generals to get them to move against the South and to keep moving against them. The President wanted a general who would take command of the situation. He believed that General Ulysses S. Grant was the man who could do it.

SECOND NARRATOR: Lincoln made Grant a lieutenant general—the army's highest rank at that time. The two men meet privately in the White House after Grant receives his commission.

LINCOLN: It was always my intention to let my generals direct the war—I am no military man—but I have been plagued by their reluctance to attack the enemy. We cannot win this war if we continue to attack and then retreat.

GRANT: The art of war is simple enough, Mr. President. Find out where your enemy is. Get at him as soon as you can. Strike at him as hard as you can and as often as you can, and keep moving on.

LINCOLN: I believe we understand each other, General Grant.

GRANT: I believe we do. But let's be clear. Do you have any special orders for me, sir?

LINCOLN: I expect you to take their capital. I expect you to take Richmond. Your country expects it of you too. Are you up to it?

GRANT: Yes, Mr. President—as long as I have enough men to back me up.

LINCOLN: Done.

GRANT: I look forward to meeting you again, sir—in Richmond, under the stars and stripes.

SCENE TWO

This scene takes place on April 7, 1865, at Lee's headquarters in the Virginia countryside.

FIRST NARRATOR: Grant devised a Grand Plan. The Union Army would coordinate its efforts and attack the Confederate Army everywhere and all at once. There would be no retreat. Grant and Meade engaged Lee in Virginia. Major General William Tecumseh Sherman marched across Georgia, capturing land, destroying rail lines, and stopping the movement of Southern supplies in the fall of 1864. Sherman's march had a terrible effect on the spirit of the Southern people.

SECOND NARRATOR: Grant's Grand Plan worked, but at a terrible price. Thousands of his men died. Still, due in part to the success of the new military strategy, Lincoln won re-election. At his inauguration, he spoke of a reunited country and offered these words of leniency to the South, "With malice toward none; with charity for all."

FIRST NARRATOR: Grant moved toward Richmond, the Confederate capital. President Jefferson Davis fled. On April 3, 1865, the American flag was over the city. Abraham Lincoln visited Richmond soon after it was taken. He was soon surrounded by a crowd of African American men, women, and children, shouting his praise.

SECOND NARRATOR: Lee moved his army west, heading for supply trains of food. Meade, with a large army, followed the Army of Northern Virginia. General Phil Sheridan and his cavalry shadowed Lee's forces, moving parallel to them on the other side of the Appomattox River.

LEE: Gentlemen, what is our situation?

LONGSTREET: We lost a third of our forces at Sayler's Creek yesterday. We now have less than 10,000 men. Today, Sheridan and his cavalry destroyed our supply trains at Appomattox Station.

GORDON: General, my men haven't eaten anything but parched corn for a month, and their uniforms are in rags—they desperately need new gear.

LEE: I was just atop the hill and saw Grant's army. Our scouts estimate that he has four men for every one of us.

GORDON: He's been willing to sacrifice his soldiers to us. We've faced such odds before.

LEE: The general dispatched this message to me *(reading):* "The result of last week must convince you of the hopelessness of further resistance. I regard it as my duty to shift from myself the responsibility of any further effusion of blood, by asking of you the surrender of that portion of the Confederate States Army known as the Army of Northern Virginia."

LONGSTREET: General—you're not considering surrender?

WISE: You must consider it. This army is hopelessly whipped. These men have already endured more than I believed flesh and blood could stand. Grant's right. If you prolong this struggle, it will be murder. The blood of every man killed from now on will be on your head. Your own son was taken prisoner yesterday. Isn't that enough?

LEE: And what would the country think of me if I surrendered?

WISE: There is no country! We haven't had a country for more than a year now. *You* are the country to these men. They have fought for you. If you demand the sacrifice, there are thousands of us who would die for you. But you know that there is no winning this. No man or government or people will question your decision to surrender.

LEE: I say that we are not done yet. There are four supply trains waiting for us at Appomattox Station. If we can reach them, then we still have a chance.

SCENE THREE
This scene takes place the same day at the headquarters of the Union Army.

GRANT: There's no word from Lee.

MEADE: We can do one of two things: We can charge the hill and smash what's left of Lee's army, or we can surround him and wait him out. Let his men starve to death.

GRANT: Lee would surrender before he let his men starve to death.

MEADE: Or he'd attack. I wouldn't put it past Lee to try to mount one more attack. He can get 50 men to fight like 5,000.

(Vincent, Meade's aide, enters the tent.)

VINCENT: General Meade, sir. General Grant, sir. Our scouts report that we're within 500 yards of the Rebels.

GRANT: Meade, I want you to take half of the army and move around to Lee's left. I'll take the other half and move around to the right. We'll surround him.

VINCENT: Sirs, may I speak?

GRANT: Go ahead, but be quick about it.

VINCENT: I fought at Chancellorsville and Gettysburg. I know how General Lee fights. He finds our weak spots and gets the most out of his men. Won't dividing our army invite General Lee to charge through our middle?

GRANT: By thunder! Stop worrying about what Robert E. Lee is thinking and start making him worry about what *we're* thinking! Understand?

VINCENT: Sir, yes, sir! I'm sorry, sir!

(Vincent leaves quickly.)

MEADE: Don't you think you were a little hard on him?

GRANT: I'll apologize to him later. But the men have to understand Lee is not running this war anymore!

SCENE FOUR

This scene takes place the next two days, April 8-9, 1865, outside of Appomattox, Virginia.

FIRST NARRATOR: General Sheridan and his Union cavalry reached Appomattox Station before Lee's army did. He was now in front of the Confederate Army.

SECOND NARRATOR: Sheridan knew his cavalry couldn't hope to stop Lee from moving forward, so he sent word to Grant to send more infantry.

LONGSTREET: We have the Union army to the east, south, and west of us. There's no food to the north of us. It would do us no good to move in that direction. Grant has us where he wants us.

LEE: Our best chance is to continue to move west. Sheridan and his cavalry can't hold us. We must strike quickly before they have a chance to reinforce. Order General Gordon to advance. I tell you, General Longstreet, I will strike that man a blow in the morning!

FIRST NARRATOR: On April 9, at dawn, the sounds of Confederate cannons and Rebel yells filled the air. The ragged, gray-suited soldiers surged into Sheridan's cavalry and were able to capture several Yankee cannons.

SECOND NARRATOR: Then the smoke cleared. A line of Union soldiers, two miles deep, stood in front of Lee's rag-tag army. Lee received news of the fight in his tent.

LONGSTREET: Here's Captain Nash!

LEE: What's your news?

NASH: I have word from General Gordon, sir.

LEE: Well, let's have it!

NASH *(reading a note):* "Tell General Lee our cannons and cavalry have dislodged the front force of the Union brigade."

LONGSTREET: Excellent! Good job, Gordon! Maybe there is hope.

LEE: Read the rest, please.

NASH: "Seeing the Union line broken we advanced. But the Unions met us with a far greater force and many of the brigade were captured. Tell General Lee I have fought my men to a frazzle, and I fear I can do nothing unless I am heavily supported by Longstreet's troops."

LONGSTREET: I'll see what I can spare—

LEE: Your men are holding our current position. The minute I move your men to Gordon's position, they'll overrun us here.

LONGSTREET: But without those supplies we can't fight—

LEE: If we move to Gordon, our entire army will be surrounded, and to what end? We'll be in exactly the same situation we are in now, maybe even worse. Too many men will die for no reason.

NASH: General Gordon ordered me to wait for an answer, General Lee.

LEE: Tell him to retreat to our position.

NASH *(sadly):* Yes, sir. *(He exits.)*

LONGSTREET: That means surrender.

LEE: There is nothing left for me to do but go and see General Grant. I would rather die a thousand deaths, but I must not surrender. The war is over.

SCENE FIVE
This scene place later in the day of April 9, 1865, outside the Appomattox Court House.

FIRST NARRATOR: General Robert E. Lee, under a white flag of truce, went to meet General Grant. Lee was dressed in his finest uniform. Arriving before Grant, Lee and his men were directed to a small brick house beside the court house.

SECOND NARRATOR: Grant rode in directly from the battlefield. In contrast to Lee, his uniform was torn and covered with mud. Union General Philip Sheridan greeted Grant when he reached the court house.

SHERIDAN: General Lee's in that brick house, waiting for you.

GRANT: Well, then, let's go over.

SHERIDAN: Have you ever met Lee?

GRANT: Once, in Mexico, during the war.

SHERIDAN: You should feel very proud today.

GRANT: I should, but I don't.

SHERIDAN: We won. We've ended the war.

GRANT: I'm relieved the fighting is over, but, by lightning, I don't see cause for celebration. Too many men are dead.

FIRST NARRATOR: Grant walked into the brick house and shook hands with General Lee. They then went into a private room to work out the surrender.

GRANT: General Lee. We meet again.

LEE: The honor is mine, General Grant.

GRANT: Please, call me Ulysses. Or Sam, if your prefer.

LEE: That's what they called you at West Point, wasn't it? Sam?

GRANT: Yes . . . that was a long time ago.

LEE: When I was the Superintendent of West Point, I worked with Major Simpson. He always spoke of you.

GRANT: Major Simpson? By thunder, he was the toughest teacher I ever had!

LEE: He rode me hard too. He never let up.

GRANT: No matter what grade I got, he always said—

GRANT AND LEE *(in unison):* "You're smart enough to do better."

GRANT: Major Simpson thought the world of you. He must have been very proud to see you as Superintendent at West Point.

LEE: What would he think if he could see us here today?

GRANT: I think he might be very proud . . . and very sad.

LEE: I suppose we should get down to business.

GRANT: General—

LEE: Robert.

GRANT: Robert. I want to apologize for the state of my uniform. I came here directly from the field—

LEE: There's no need to apologize.

GRANT: Do you remember when we met in Mexico, in front of General Scott's tent? You wouldn't let me see the general because my uniform was dirty.

LEE: That was a long time ago. You've earned the right to wear your uniform proudly.

GRANT: I've never forgotten that meeting.

LEE: Shall we get down to business?

GRANT: Of course.

SECOND NARRATOR: General Grant and General Lee worked out the terms of surrender of the Confederate Army, effectively ending the Civil War. Grant continued to talk about their days at West Point, and more than once Lee had to get him back on the subject.

FIRST NARRATOR: The terms of agreement had been worked out with President Lincoln on board the riverboat *River Queen* on March 28, 1865. Lincoln wanted the Confederate army disarmed and then allowed to go home.

GRANT: Your officers will keep their weapons and horses.

LEE: Most of my soldiers own their own horses.

GRANT: I don't see any problems with the soldiers keeping their horses too. They'll most likely need them to put in a crop.

LEE: Thank you.

GRANT: Any other concerns?

LEE: My men are starving. They need food.

GRANT: We have rations for about 25,000 men. I'll order the supplies released to your soldiers.

LEE: Thank you. Although I wish it had been under different circumstances, I'm glad to have met you again, General Grant.

GRANT: It has been an honor to see you, General Lee. I thought when we did meet, we would be on the same side.

LEE: I had hoped for the same thing. May we never have to fight each other again.

GRANT: That is my prayer too.

LEE: Here is my sword, as a symbol of surrender.

GRANT: No, sir. The war's over now. We're all Americans again. The only thing I will ask for is your hand in friendship.

SECOND NARRATOR: Grant and Lee shook hands on their agreement, and then returned to their armies. The War Between the States was over.

FIRST NARRATOR: Although there were tough days ahead for the United States, Americans began the work of knitting together their torn nation. That effort started on April 9, 1865, when two officers—allies who became enemies—shook hands. The spirit of Appomattox set the stage for the healing to come. Lincoln's hope for a gentle peace seemed destined to occur.

Background on Grant and Lee

Robert E. Lee was born in Stratford, Virginia, in 1807. Ulysses Simpson Grant was born in Point Pleasant, Ohio, in 1822. Their military careers are full of remarkable parallels. Both were graduates of West Point—Lee graduated second in his class in 1829 and was considered a brilliant student with a great future in the military. Grant, who graduated in 1843, was 21st in a class of 39 and thought of as a bright but lazy student who had trouble focusing on his studies.

Both served in the Mexican War. Lee received three battlefield promotions, was wounded at the battle of Chapultepec in 1847, and distinguished himself with his inventive strategies which, it would turn out, were years ahead of their time. His experience identified him to General Winfield Scott and other officers as a future great general. Grant also distinguished himself at the battle of Chapultepec, but did not receive the attention of his superiors and by 1854 had resigned from the Army, claiming loneliness and a drinking problem.

Lee went on to become superintendent of West Point and, when it appeared hostilities were about to break out between the North and the South, was offered command of the entire Union army by President Abraham Lincoln. But Virginia was about to secede, so Lee declined Lincoln's offer so he could serve in Virginia's militia. Lee was named commander-in-chief of Virginia's forces. Grant, who by now was living in Illinois with his wife Julia, joined the Illinois Volunteers when the Civil War broke out.

It was during the Civil War that the fortunes of the two men began to turn. Lee was hopelessly outnumbered and outgunned from the start, yet his brilliant strategic maneuvers led to many early Confederate victories. It was not until he was repulsed at Gettysburg that tide turned away from the Confederate army. Grant, through his victories at the battles of Shiloh and Vicksburg, was given command of all the Union armies. "I cannot spare this man," Lincoln said of Grant, "he fights!" Knowing he could not outsmart Lee or defeat him strategically, Grant became the first Union commander to use his army's advantages in men and weapons by applying relentless pressure against Lee and the Virginia armies.

By April 1865 Grant's plan had worked. Lee's army was worn out, depleted, and starving. Grant, wanting no more bloodshed, asked for Lee's surrender. But Lee was a master at outsmarting his enemy and deploying troops in such a way that his small army could defeat a much larger one. He tried one last time to break the Union line,

but his troops were just too weary. With no other course, Lee surrendered to Grant on April 9, 1865. According to Lee's memoirs, when he finally met General Grant again, their conversation was so pleasant they forgot for a brief moment why they were meeting. Lee had to continually return Grant to the subject.

Lee went on to become President of Washington College, which today is Washington and Lee University. He died in 1870. Grant, hailed as a national hero, was elected President of the United States in 1868. He eventually settled in New York, where he died in 1885.

Book Links

Archer, Jules. *A House Divided: The Lives of Ulysses S. Grant and Robert E. Lee.* New York: Scholastic, 1997.

Fleming, Thomas. *Band of Brothers: West Point in the Civil War.* New York: Walker and Company, 1988.

Grant, Ulysses S. *Personal Memoirs of Ulysses S. Grant and Selected Letters, 1839-1865.* New York: The Library of America, 1990.

Smith, Carter, ed. *The Road to Appomattox: A Sourcebook on the Civil War.* Brookfield CT: The Millbrook Press, 1995.

Classroom Discussion and Activities

DISCUSSION QUESTIONS

• Read aloud the following quote to students, or write it on the board: "In this enlightened age, slavery as an institution is a moral, political evil in any country." (They were written by Robert E. Lee before the outbreak of the Civil War.) What are students' reactions when you reveal the author of the quote? Talk about their reactions. Then discuss the dilemma Lee faced when Abraham Lincoln offered him command of the Union army. Why do they think Lee didn't take Lincoln's offer? Do students think Lee's decision to turn it down was wrong? Encourage them to justify their reasoning. As an extension, direct students to find out how officers on both sides of the conflict personally felt about slavery and secession. What were these men's reasons for joining the Union or Confederate armies?

• Tell students that Lee was superintendent of West Point from 1852 until Jefferson Davis, who was Secretary of War under President Franklin Pierce, transferred Lee to head the 2nd Cavalry in Texas. Lee attended West Point too—as did officers on both sides of the Civil War including Grant, Meade, Longstreet, Ewell, Jeb Stuart, Hooker, and Pickett. Many of these men fought together in the Mexican War under the American flag. Ask students if they think going to military school and fighting in a war together was an advantage or disadvantage to the Northern and Southern officers and to explain why or why not. Urge students to consider the emotional aspects of these relationships as well as the military aspects.

ACTIVITIES

Last Thoughts Before the Meeting Have students imagine they are either General Grant or General Lee on the morning of April 9 and then write a diary entry about the upcoming meeting of surrender. They should Include their feelings about the opposing general, about meeting him, about the surrender, and about the future—theirs, their men's, and the country's.

News of the Day Suggest that students "cover" Lee's and Grant's meeting as reporters. Like good reporters, they should research both men and review the events of the Civil War to prepare for the historic meeting between the two generals. Students may write newspaper articles describing the meeting or choose to "interview" one or both men. You may also want to let students perform the play and then have those who are not in the cast act as reporters. Add a scene to end of the play where Grant and Lee hold a press conference and the reporters question them. The reporters will then write their newspaper articles.

The Civil War at Home Set aside time for students to view all or part of *The Civil War*, Ken Burns' award-winning PBS video. After the viewing, talk about what kinds of sources Burns used in the documentary. Challenge students to plan their own documentary based on what was happening in their region of the country during the Civil War. Hold a class brain-storming session about how to find sources in their own community about that time period. Guide students as necessary. For instance, alert them if your town has a historical association or your public library has an archivist. Remind them to ask their parents and other relatives about stories they might know. When students compile and sort their information, encourage them to begin writing a script.

The Fate of Robert E. Lee's Home Arlington House, Robert E. Lee's home in Virginia, was taken over by Federal forces in 1861. In addition to being a military headquarters for the Union army, the Freedman's Bureau built a Freedman's Village on the grounds where about 2,000 African Americans lived. Today it is the site of Arlington National Cemetery. Have students research and report on one aspect of Arlington's history.

A HARD PEACE

Abraham Lincoln and the Reconstruction

JOHN WILKES BOOTH

ANDREW JOHNSON

CAST
(in order of appearance)

First Narrator

Second Narrator

John Wilkes Booth: Actor and Southern sympathizer

Lewis Paine: Former Confederate private

Abraham Lincoln: Sixteenth President of the United States

Edwin M. Stanton: United States Secretary of War

General Ulysses S. Grant: Commander of the Union Army

Mary Todd Lincoln: Abraham Lincoln's wife

Messenger

Dr. Charles A. Leale: U.S. Army surgeon

Andrew Johnson: Lincoln's Vice President

Olivia Wilson: Emancipated African American woman living in Georgia

Thomas Wilson: Olivia's husband

SCENE ONE
This scene takes place on April 10, 1865, on the White House lawn.

FIRST NARRATOR: The Southern states of Louisiana, Arkansas, and Tennessee were occupied by Federal troops before the Civil War was over. Lincoln issued the Proclamation of Amnesty and Reconstruction on December 8, 1863. In the proclamation, he declared what the three Southern states—and eventually all the Southern states—could do to rejoin the Union.

SECOND NARRATOR: Lincoln said that he would pardon "all persons who have . . . participated in the existing rebellion" except for officials of the Confederate government, Federal judges who had left the bench and senators and representatives who had left Congress to join the South, and high-ranking Confederate military officers. Pardons would be granted as long as the person signed an oath of loyalty to the United States.

FIRST NARRATOR: In the proclamation, Lincoln didn't insist upon suffrage for African American men or that property owned by former slaveholders be distributed among newly freed slaves. Some people didn't believe that the proclamation went far enough. Others, like John Wilkes Booth, thought it went too far.

SECOND NARRATOR: As news of the fall of Richmond and Lee's surrender at Appomattox spread, crowds began to gather on the White House lawn. They cheered for Lincoln and waited for some words from the President. What kind of reconstruction plans would Lincoln announce now? John Wilkes Booth and Lewis Paine were in the crowd.

JOHN WILKES BOOTH: We'll get him. We still have a chance. Lee might have surrendered but Joseph Johnston hasn't. He's got at least 30,000 men with him in North Carolina. He'll hold out, don't you worry.

LEWIS PAINE (*looking around uneasily*): You'd better watch your words. You're not exactly surrounded by loving fans.

JOHN WILKES BOOTH: But I am. If they haven't seen me on stage, then they've seen my picture hundreds of times in the newspaper or on playbills.

LEWIS PAINE: All the more reason you should watch your words.

JOHN WILKES BOOTH: What? I shouldn't say that I'd be willing trade Honest Abe for all the Southern soldiers being held in Yankee prisons? All the South needs is more men. One tall, ugly Yankee president for hundreds of thousands of Southern soldiers—that's a fair trade. We'll see then whether the war's over or not. I'm willing to make sure it happens.

LEWIS PAINE: So am I, but I don't want the whole world to find out about it before it happens.

JOHN WILKES BOOTH: All we have to do is watch and wait for our chance.

FIRST NARRATOR: The crowd erupted into cheers and wild applause as the doors to an upper balcony of the White House opened and President Lincoln stepped out. The cheering went on for several minutes, but finally, with the light of a candle, Lincoln began reading from handwritten notes.

ABRAHAM LINCOLN: "We meet this evening, not in sorrow, but in gladness of heart. The evacuation of Petersburg and Richmond, and the surrender of the principal insurgent army, give hope of a righteous and speedy peace whose joyous expression can not be restrained."

JOHN WILKES BOOTH: A righteous peace! Coming from the North? There's not such thing!

ABRAHAM LINCOLN: "We all agree that the seceding States, so called, are out their proper practical relation with the Union; and that the sole object of the government, civil and military, in regard to these States is to again get them into that proper practical relation. I believe it is not only possible, but in fact, easier, to do this, without deciding, or even considering, whether these states have been out of the Union, than with it. Finding themselves safely at home, it would be utterly immaterial whether they had ever been abroad. "

JOHN WILKES BOOTH: Do you hear him? Do you hear him reducing us to *tourists?* Thousands of us have died fighting for the rightness of our cause, and he compares secession to taking a boat ride across the Atlantic!

LEWIS PAINE: Sshh!

ABRAHAM LINCOLN: "Now, if we reject the people of Louisiana and their new state government, and spurn them, we do our utmost to disorganize and disperse them. We in effect say to the white men 'You are worthless, or worse—we will neither help you, nor be helped by you.' To the blacks we say 'This cup of liberty which these, your old masters, hold to your lips, we will dash from you, and leave you to the chances of gathering the spilled and scattered contents in some vague and undefined when, where, and how.'"

JOHN WILKES BOOTH: Black lips will never, ever, touch the cup of liberty, Old Abe. I promise you that.

ABRAHAM LINCOLN: "I repeat the question. 'Can Louisiana be brought into proper practical relation with the Union sooner by *sustaining* or by *discarding* her new State Government?' What has been said of Louisiana will apply generally to other States. And yet so great peculiarities pertain to each state; and such important and sudden changes occur in the same state; . . . that no exclusive and inflexible plan can safely be prescribed. "

JOHN WILKES BOOTH: That is the last speech he will ever make—I swear!

LEWIS PAINE: What are you going to do? Booth?

SCENE TWO
This scene takes place on April 14, 1865, at a Cabinet meeting in the White House.

ABRAHAM LINCOLN: How's Mr. Seward today?

EDWIN M. STANTON: Still in a great deal of pain. He comes and goes out of delirium.

GENERAL GRANT: A broken arm and a jaw broken in two places will do that.

EDWIN M. STANTON: Jumping out of an out-of-control carriage will do that. No word from Sherman yet in regard to Johnston's surrender?

ABRAHAM LINCOLN: Not yet.

EDWIN M. STANTON: There is the question of what to do with Jeff Davis and his Confederates once we catch them.

ABRAHAM LINCOLN: I hope there will be no persecution, no bloody work after the war is over. No one need expect me to take any part in hanging or killing these men, even the worst of them. Frighten them out of the country; open the gates; let down the bars. *(waving his fingers)* Shoo; scare them off; enough lives have been sacrificed.

EDWIN M. STANTON: As for reconstructing the South, we'll need to send in Union troops at first.

ABRAHAM LINCOLN: We can't undertake to run state governments in all these southern states. Their people must do that—though I reckon that at first some of them may do it badly. *(standing up)* Well, gentlemen, thank you for your time. General Grant, my wife and I look forward to seeing you tonight.

GENERAL GRANT: Unfortunately, sir, I must break our engagement. Julia and I are leaving for New Jersey to meet our children.

ABRAHAM LINCOLN: Another time then—the children must come first.

FIRST NARRATOR: After the Cabinet members left, Lincoln sat alone in the Oval Office. Mary Todd entered the room and found her husband staring out the window.

MARY TODD LINCOLN: What are you thinking, Abraham?

ABRAHAM LINCOLN: Mary! I didn't hear you come in.

MARY TODD LINCOLN: You seemed very far away, staring out that window.

ABRAHAM LINCOLN: I'm very worried about the country, Mary. General Lee has surrendered and the shooting has stopped, but I'm afraid the fighting between us will go on. How will the South deal with the freed slaves when they're citizens? They've looked upon black people as their property for so long, will they now be

able to think of them as neighbors? We've kept the country together by force of the army, and now the South is defeated.

MARY TODD LINCOLN: It's going to take some time for the wounds to heal, Abraham. You know that. You've always known that.

ABRAHAM LINCOLN: That's just it. I don't know how much time we have.

MARY TODD LINCOLN: You've done all you can, Abraham, at least for right now. Today, there are no battles being fought. No men are dying. Husbands are returning to their wives, fathers to their children. Those are *good things,* Abraham. Healing things. The politics of this peace will work themselves out. And I know you, you won't leave the vulnerable unprotected. When the United States woke up this morning, it was not at war. The nation has you to thank for that.

ABRAHAM LINCOLN *(smiling):* I reckon I could stand a little rejoicing.

MARY TODD LINCOLN: I reckon you could. That's why we're absolutely going to the theater tonight.

SCENE THREE
This scene takes place that same evening at Ford's Theater.

SECOND NARRATOR: As an actor, John Wilkes Booth had spent many hours at Ford's Theater. He could come and go, prowling around the theater, without anyone thinking his behavior was odd.

FIRST NARRATOR: President Lincoln and his wife Mary arrived at the theater late, at about 8:30. The play had already started. John Wilkes Booth entered the theater at about 10:00. He made his way to the presidential box. Booth stood behind Lincoln and shot the President behind his left ear. Abraham Lincoln slumped in his chair.

MARY TODD LINCOLN: Abraham? What is it?

JOHN WILKES BOOTH: Freedom!

MARY TODD LINCOLN: Abraham! Help! Someone help!

JOHN WILKES BOOTH: *Sic semper tyrannis!* Thus always to tyrants!

SECOND NARRATOR: Booth pulled a knife. He fought with and wounded Major Henry Rathbone, who was also sitting in the box. Then Booth jumped out of the box, landing 12 feet below on the stage and breaking his left leg.

FIRST NARRATOR: Despite his injuries, Booth managed to escape from the theater. Many people in the audience thought the shot, Mrs. Lincoln's screams, and Booth's leap to the stage were part of the performance. But soon everyone inside Ford's Theater knew that the President had been shot, perhaps fatally.

SCENE FOUR

This scene takes place that night at Edwin Stanton's at about the same time as the previous scene. A violent knocking on the front door awakens Stanton.

MESSENGER: Secretary Stanton! Secretary Stanton! Wake up, sir!

EDWIN M. STANTON: Yes, yes, what is it?

MESSENGER: Sir, I have terrible news! Secretary Seward has been attacked in his home!

EDWIN M. STANTON: What?! What happened? Is he all right?

MESSENGER: He's wounded, sir, but alive. A man—he said he was from the doctor, he had medicine for Mr. Seward—he forced his way into the house. Mr. Seward's son attacked the man but was wounded. There were other injuries—

EDWIN M. STANTON: Did they catch the man?

MESSENGER: No sir.

EDWIN M. STANTON: Get a carriage for me! Quickly!

SECOND NARRATOR: At Seward's house, Stanton heard the news about the President. He rode immediately to the boarding house across from the theater where Lincoln had been taken. The president's oldest son Robert sat with his father. Mary Todd and her younger son Tad were in the next room. Stanton left the President's bedside to meet with the young Army surgeon Dr. Charles A. Leale. The doctor had been at Ford's Theater and had rushed to the President's aid.

EDWIN M. STANTON: What are you doing to save him? You must save him! You must!

DR. CHARLES A. LEALE: All we can do now is keep him comfortable. He doesn't have much time left. He's lost too much blood.

EDWIN M. STANTON: Do you know what this means for the country? You must save him.

DR. CHARLES A. LEALE: Mr. Secretary, there's nothing more that we can do.

EDWIN M. STANTON: That's unacceptable, doctor. When you have something positive to report, let me know. I'll be in that bedroom there. You, there! Follow me!

MESSENGER (*following Stanton into the room*): Yes sir?

EDWIN M. STANTON: Take this down: I want guards posted outside the residences of all Cabinet members. I want all southbound passenger trains out of Washington stopped. I forbid any boat on the Potomac to touch the southern shore. I want all troops in Washington and the fire brigade on alert. Find out who's taking down the testimony of the witnesses and get the notes to me. One last thing—

MESSENGER: Sir?

EDWIN M. STANTON: Shut down Ford's Theater.

FIRST NARRATOR: By 3:00 the next morning, cables identifying John Wilkes Booth as the assassin were being sent out. Abraham Lincoln died that morning, April 15, at 7:22. Stanton delivered the awful news to the crowd gathered in the rain around the boarding house.

SCENE FIVE
This scene takes place on April 15, 1865, at the White House in Washington, D.C.

SECOND NARRATOR: After Lincoln's death, Vice President Andrew Johnson was sworn in as President of the United States on April 15, 1865.

FIRST NARRATOR: Although Johnson was from Tennessee, he had stayed with the Union instead of joining the Confederacy.

EDWIN M. STANTON: Mr. President, the task of reconstructing the South is in your hands.

ANDREW JOHNSON: And you wonder what my views—as a man from Tennessee—are on the subject?

EDWIN M. STANTON: The government must continue to run, especially now. We must not show the South that it has won anything by killing our President.

ANDREW JOHNSON: The South did not kill the President. One man—John Wilkes Booth—is responsible for his death. As for my sympathies, you need not worry. I have no love for the plantation owners. I am for the common man—or the common white man, should I say.

EDWIN M. STANTON: Stevens and the other Radical Republicans in the Congress will call on your to give citizenship and the vote to the black man. If you resist, you will be in for a fight.

ANDREW JOHNSON: I don't mind a fight—especially when I am in the right. They can send me as many bills as they want. I'll veto them all.

EDWIN M. STANTON: President Lincoln favored the advice of his Cabinet. He appreciated exploring all the different turns that an issue may have—

ANDREW JOHNSON: All issues have only one side, Mr. Stanton—my side.

SCENE SIX
This scene takes place at a house in rural Georgia in April 1867.

SECOND NARRATOR: And so, the harsh peace the North sought to impose on the South began. The Senate passed amendments outlawing slavery and secession, took away homes and land belonging to the Southerners, gave the freed slaves their citizenship, put parts of the South under military rule, and paved the way for Northerners, called "carpetbaggers" to come South and buy Southern land from the government at cheap prices. President Johnson vetoed these bills. His vetoes were overridden.

FIRST NARRATOR: Some of the people these bills were meant to help were still worried.

OLIVIA WILSON: Says here in the paper, we've going to get the right to vote.

THOMAS WILSON: That's not all the news. I have a piece of land all picked out. Soon as I get some work, we're going to buy it.

OLIVIA WILSON: Who are you kidding? Do you know what I heard the other day? Some Confederate officers are forming groups, groups that go out at night and wear white sheets over their heads and burn down our homes. They find any of us trying to get other colored people to vote, they take him and hang him from a tree.

THOMAS WILSON: Oh, Olivia, don't get yourself worked up over nothing. There's always going to be a few bad men floating around.

OLIVIA WILSON: A few bad men? This is an organized army! What do you think they spent the last four years fighting for?

THOMAS WILSON: We're citizens now. The government has to protect us.

OLIVIA WILSON: Oh? Government going to follow you everywhere you go? Government going to go with every colored man who wants to vote? You think so?

THOMAS WILSON: You look for trouble everywhere.

OLIVIA WILSON: Everybody thinks its going to get easier for the colored people now that the Yankees have won. But you can't take the dignity of a man away without that man fighting back. And who are those white Southern men going to fight back against? They can't fight back against the Yankees, they already lost to them. They're smart enough so they won't fight against each other. All they can do is fight the colored people, because they got to fight somebody.

THOMAS WILSON: I sure wish Mr. Lincoln was still living. He knew how a man's heart worked. You treat a man like a child, you take his dignity away. You take his dignity away, you make him mad. You make him mad, he has to find somebody to strike out against.

OLIVIA WILSON: I just hope we can hang on to this freedom. I don't like this hard peace.

SECOND NARRATOR: Olivia was right. Some wondered if the hard peace really helped anyone. The Ku Klux Klan, formed by former Confederate officers, terrorized freed slaves. Southern states passed the Black Codes—laws enacted in the Southern states aimed at keeping African Americans from voting, holding the same jobs as whites, staying in the same hotels, or using the same facilities—everything from schools to drinking fountains. These laws would stay in effect for almost 100 years, until 1969, when they were repealed.

FIRST NARRATOR: But the country did hold together and survive. The war was fought to keep America united, and it remains so today.

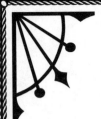

BACKGROUND AND CLASSROOM GUIDE

Background on Lincoln's Assassination and Reconstruction

As early as 1863, President Lincoln began to wrestle with the problem of how to re-admit the Confederate states to the Union. During the war, he devised a plan that would allow a state to rejoin the United States if, after being occupied by Union troops, ten percent of the property-owning men took a loyalty oath to the United States and acknowledged the outlawing of slavery. These ten percent could then vote and elect a new state government. Lincoln's plan became known as the "10% Plan." It was widely criticized as being too lenient on the South, since it allowed the Southerners to set up their own governments and did not address the problem of the freed slaves.

The plan came to a halt on April 15, 1865. Lincoln was attending a play with his wife Mary, when he was shot and killed by John Wilkes Booth, an actor and Southern sympa-thizer. Like many Southerners, Booth thought of Lincoln as a tyrant, even though his peace terms were milder than many Northerners wanted. Lincoln died the next day, and one of the results of his death was that the plans for Reconstruction were thrown into chaos.

Without a strong leader in the White House, those wanting to impose a harsh peace on the South had no one standing in their way. The 10% plan was abandoned and, with many Southern states passing laws that kept the freed slaves from owning property or exercising their right to vote, Congress began a more aggressive Reconstruction policy. This policy featured appointment of governors by the Federal Government (rather than by election); denial of representa-tion in Congress for Southern states until they accepted the 13th, 14th, and 15th Amendments, guaranteed the freed slaves the right to vote; and permanently barred Confederates from the new state governments.

While the harsh Reconstruction plan did guarantee rights to the freed slaves and forever outlawed slavery, it also built up resentments between North and South, as well as between whites and blacks. It led to the rise of the Ku Klux Klan, as well as the enactment of laws in the South—Black Codes—that barred African Americans from owning businesses or property or from sharing public facilities with whites. Many of these policies stayed in effect for the next hundred years.

Book Links

Calvert, Patricia. *Sooner.* New York: Atheneum, 1998.

Freedman, Russell. *Lincoln: A Photobiography.* New York: Clarion, 1989.

Hansen, Joyce. *I Thought My Soul Would Rise and Fly: The Diary of Patsy, a Freed Girl.* New York: Scholastic, 1997.

Smith, John David. *Black Voices from Reconstruction: 1865-1877.* Brookfield, CT: The Millbrook Press, 1996.

Classroom Discussion Activities

DISCUSSION QUESTIONS

• Historians always wrestle with "what if" questions. Have the class work in small groups and discuss how Reconstruction might have been different if President Lincoln had not been assassinated. Tell students to be as specific as possible and to give several examples. For instance, urge them to think about whether or not the Southern states would have been able to pass the Black Codes, and how that might have affected the civil rights movement of this century. Allow time for the groups to present their conclusions to the class and discuss them.

• Ask students to imagine that they were part of Lincoln's Cabinet. What kind of reconstruction would they have recommended for the Southern states? Would they favor a lenient peace or a harsh one?

ACTIVITIES

The Death of Lincoln Lincoln's assassination profoundly affected Americans. Direct students to find out what the responses of some of the people in the these plays were to the President's death. What did Mary Chestnut write in her diary about the assassination? How did Frederick Douglass take the news? How did the various Confederate and the Union officers feel? Urge students to expand their research to include other Americans—Walt Whitman, for example, as well as ordinary citizens. Collect the responses in a scrapbook. Encourage students to include text as well as photographs of Lincoln and the people who spoke and wrote about him.

Abraham Lincoln and Andrew Johnson Based upon their reading of this play, what are students' reactions to Andrew Johnson? How would they compare his style of leadership to Abraham Lincoln's? List students' comments on the board. Then direct them to find out more about the man who succeeded Lincoln. Give students the option of presenting their research in the form of a play. The entire class can work on the outline for the play, deciding how many scenes there should be and what the focus of each scene should be. Different groups of students can write the different scenes. Stage a reading of the play for other classes and/or family and friends.

Editorial Comments Assign the following task to students: Write a newspaper editorial for a newspaper that came out the day after the war ended. Be sure to address some of the following issues: What do you think the future of the United States will be? Will the country come back together, or is there a possibility of another war? What should happen to the newly emancipated African Americans? What should happen to the officers and soldiers of the Confederate army?

The Two Sides of Reconstruction Reconstruction went through two phases, Presidential Reconstruction and Congressional Reconstruction. Guide students in researching these two phases. Once their research is finished, ask them to help you create a lesson plan for teaching reconstruction. What points would they cover? In what sequence would they present the points? What kinds of material would they use to present the information? What would they do to make the lesson exciting and informative?

ABOUT THE AUTHOR

Timothy Nolan is the author of the plays *Under the Green Ceiling; Acts of Contrition; The Bull Ring; What's In A Name; Pop's Closet; Another Sunday Dinner; Applaud, Friends; Button Man; Sweetness;* and *Hoffman Boys;* the screenplays *Green Christmas and White Trash.* His work has appeared in the collections of readers' theater plays *Famous Americans,* and he is the author of *Plays About the Presidents* (both published by Scholastic Professional Books). He is a co-founder of Present Tense Productions, a member of the Dramatists Guild, and was in residence at the T. Schreiber Studios for five years. He lives in Brooklyn, New York with his wife, the playwright Susannah Nolan, their daughter Olivia Rose, and their cats Rosalind and Louisa.